What People Say About *DOWN UNDER ALL OVER:* W9-BBQ-201

Barbara Brewster writes about Australia with a lover's indulgence and passion, tempered by a keen eye for the idiosyncratic nature of both the country and its inhabitants. If the stories that this American-born self-confessed Australiaphile relates convince some doubting Aussies that this land is indeed one of the best spots on earth to live, then she'll be proved to be a fair dinkum beaut shiela, no worries.
ERIC BOGLE, Australian singer and song writer.

Down Under All Over shows a remarkable sense of love and perception for things Australian...My greatest dream is that through the love of the nature of Australia, people from all backgrounds, races and cultures will come together. Belief simply in the "SPIRIT OF THE LAND" is slowly but surely bringing the ancient Aboriginal culture and the "NEW WORLD" together. Australia has the chance to shake off the shackles of antiquated outlooks and to emerge as the great land in the south, glowing with love and respect for all living things...**Barbara Brewster** is part of this process; passing the message on to the world.
JOHN WILLIAMSON, Australian singer and song writer.

Goodonyer Barbara! Loved your book. She's a little beauty. Tell all your Yankee mates to head Down Under--the place of "No Worries." Tell them I'll buy their first beer in Alice.
TED EGAN, Australian singer and song writer.

Down Under All Over is more than a travelogue. It is an account of Barbara Brewster's very personal journey--one which entices us to follow along in her footsteps through that fascinating land of Australia. Her account of the adventures she and her husband, Sid, shared invites one to crawl under the skin of the land and to know its colloquialisms and people. Brewster's enthusiasm for the place is contagious.
SHARON and GARY DAVIDSON, authors of "Europe With Two Kids and a Van."

Barbara Brewster's vignettes of Australia are marvelous! She is a spectacularly good writer!

MICHAEL PAGE--Editor (Retired), Rigby's Publishers, Australia.

As a travel agent, I've been sending people to Australia for years. Now, for the first time, I'm inspired to want to go there myself. I want to give copies of *Down Under All Over* to all my Australian-bound clients.

SUSAN CAIRNS--Manager, Applause Travel, Portland, Oregon.

Down Under All Over shows how an individual can become a participant in the heartbeat of a country, and how, when one brings an attitude of curiosity, openness, flexibility and contribution, the doors can open upon rich and wondrous adventures.

Mike Gotesman, Master Social Worker, Beaverton, Oregon.

Reading this charming book is as enjoyable as a trip to Australia. The descriptions are so vividly painted that I felt as if I were right there seeing the land, hearing its sounds and smelling the air.

May Waldrup: Owner, Thunderbird Bookstore, Carmel, California.

Never in my wildest imagination did I have the slightest hint of an interest in Australia. Now that I've read *Down Under All Over*, I want to go there.

Carol Erdman, Editor, WHATEVER Publishing, Portland, Oregon.

DOWN UNDER ALL OVER

A LOVE AFFAIR WITH AUSTRALIA

by

BARBARA MARIE BREWSTER

Four Winds Publications

ACKNOWLEDGEMENTS

Some of these articles have been published in the following Australian newspapers and magazines: *The Northern Guardian, The Naracoorte Herald, The Broome News, The Coober Pedy Times, INSECT; The Journal of the South East Cultural Trust.* In the United States *The Dolphins of Monkey Mia* appeared in *The Transformation Times*, Portland, Oregon.

The people and places mentioned in this book are real. Some names have been changed, however, to honor the privacy of those concerned.

AUSTRALIAN TERMS

Throughout the book I have indicated with an * those terms which may be unfamiliar to American readers. These are listed and defined in the Glossary. All prices are quoted in Australian dollars, unless otherwise specified.

COVER PHOTO

Cover Photo shows a boab tree, photographed at the Zoological Gardens in Broome, on the north coast of Western Australia. The bulbous shape of the "bottle tree" stores water, enabling it to survive long dry spells. These fairytale-looking trees are entirely huggable.

Copyright   Barbara Marie Brewster, 1991. All rights reserved.

Publishers Cataloging in Publication (*Prepared by Quality Books Inc.*)

Brewster, Barbara Marie, 1944-
   Down Under all over: a love affair with Australia / by Barbara Marie Brewster.--
      p. cm.
   Includes bibliographical references.
   ISBN 0-9628608-0-8
   1. Australia--Description and travel--1981- 2. Australia--History. 3. Brewster, Barbara
Marie, 1944-   I. Title.

DU105   994   QB191-1297
                                                              MARC

Four Winds Publishing
P.O. Box 19033, Portland, Oregon, 97219, USA
Phone or Fax 503 246-9424

FOREWORD

It is truly a joy to find someone who has written about my home with such love, affection and understanding of its true values. In *Down Under All Over*, I feel, almost, as if Barbara Brewster is putting down my own innermost thoughts and feelings about the country I love. Obviously, she loves Australia too. The love comes through the ordinary text to such an extent that I found myself with eyes filled with tears that someone from another country had so clearly got the essential "gist" of what Australia is about, had managed to grab the fundamental spirit of the place, to write about it with such ease, and...anyway...what can I say? I love it!

Barbara Brewster should be declared an honorary Australian! Great stuff!!

"Tie Me Kangaroo Down Sport" Rolf Harris

CONTENTS

CONTENTS

*From Albany to Halls Creek, from Uluru to Yanaki, countless welcoming Australians shared themselves, their country and their hearts with Sid and me. It is their spirits which infuse the pages of this book and which have brought it to life. **Down Under All Over** is for them, with my thanks.*

*It is also for Sid,
who kept the car, the computer, and the dream afloat.*

PREFACE

A DREAM COMES TRUE--TWICE

MY LOVE AFFAIR with Australia goes back as far as I can remember. Since childhood I have memorized Australia's songs and poems, seen movies like *The Sundowners* several times over, and have been fascinated by her history, people and land. In my young imagination Australia embodied the qualities of a "last frontier" and a way of life that was rapidly vanishing from the United States. I now believe that Australia has reached out and touched me at some core level of my consciousness, one that I can comprehend only superficially.

I grew up in a small California town where I roamed the hillsides on horseback and afoot, hunting, hiking or driving cattle on friends' ranches. With my family, I travelled the United States and Alaska, camping and backpacking in deserts, mountains and parks. I thrived on the open-aired freedom and the demand of robust country, relishing such heady refreshments as splashing in a cool river or cattle trough on hot days and savoring the contrast of cleanliness after periods of hardy, dirt-stained activity.

"Australia will be like this," I always thought.

When I was in high school my family applied to have an American Field Service student live with us for one year. Out of a whole world of applicants, an Australian girl, Diana, was assigned to us. In that year of living like sisters, the seeds were sown for the harvest of adventures that were yet to come.

After Diana returned to Australia in 1963, I began what was to become a rather erratic and drawn-out college career. No matter how much I enjoyed my two years at the University of California at Davis, an enchanting year of studying in Denmark, and a stint at the Institute of Foreign Studies in spectacular Monterey, California, the call of Australia persisted like a strong undercurrent beneath the surface of my days.

Throughout the spring of 1967, I researched options. If I wasn't bombarding the Australian Consulate with letters seeking information, I was bouncing in and out of their offices in San Francisco. I learned that Australia had a population of only 10 million people and was avidly recruiting new settlers. My decision was made.

I began to make plans. To save money, I installed a roommate in my apartment and took a part-time secretarial job. I applied for a visa and booked passage on a P&O liner-- all without telling my parents. I knew they would be dismayed about my decision. Reluctant to hurt and disappoint them, I delayed telling them as long as I could.

When the school year started in September and I did not enroll, I finally revealed my plans to my parents. My father rallied quickly, and there was a twinkle in his eyes when he said he now had a reason to visit Australia. My mother did not fare so well. The woman who had always encouraged me to travel while I was young, and who, as a single school teacher had periodically gone into debt in order to see the world, now was chiefly concerned about how to explain me to her friends.

Finally all the pieces began to fit together. I immigrated on *The Assisted Passage Scheme*--which meant that in return for remaining in the country for a minimum of two years, Australia would pay nearly half of my fare. On November 18, 1967, *The Himalaya* docked in Sydney Cove. I was there.

Since I didn't know a soul in Sydney, I was bowled over to hear my name blared over the ship's loudspeaker. When I answered the page, I came face to face with two officials from the Immigration Department who had come to meet me. They offered to help me with my Sydney accommodations as well as to pay my way to whatever destination I chose.

"Keith, South Australia," I said, without hesitation. Diana lived there with her husband, a grazier*. Her welcoming letters, which reached me on board the ship, urged me to hurry to "Stirling," their sheep property, in time to attend the annual Black and White Ball. I'd never been to a ball and wasn't about to pass up this one. After staying with some ship acquaintances in Sydney for a few days, I boarded the train for Keith and embarked on my life Down Under.

It was an incredible period, a time when the country welcomed both immigrants and "Yanks"--and I was part of it. Doors opened wherever I went, and jobs, friends, amazing experiences rushed up to greet me. Like the country, I was growing, flexing my muscles, trying new things and developing my own style.

Australia was so eager for teachers that my motley but diverse education (which included no teacher training whatsoever) landed me a job as a teacher in the Keith School. From Keith I foraged out on weekends and school holidays, hitchhiking, exploring and adventuring. At the end of the year, rich in new friends whom I left behind, I hitched across the continent to Perth--no mean feat in 1969, for much of the transcontinental "highway" was still a dirt road. I loved it, and when I got to Perth, I loved that too.

In the years that followed, my tracks took me all over the state of Western Australia, from Albany in the south to Broome in the north. Back in the east, I hitched around Tasmania, across Queensland, through the Center, up to Darwin and on into Asia, then back again to Australia. During that time, first my parents and later my sister came to Australia. They all loved the country and were welcomed and warmed in the glow of my special Australian friends.

There came a time, however, when my wandering no longer sufficed. In the course of four years I had tried different jobs, highways, experiences and relationships, but I wasn't satisfied. As much as I thrilled to and thrived on my vagabond life, there was a part of me that was incomplete and unfulfilled. I decided to stop wandering--to slip into a more structured skin, and complete my university degree. *Then* perhaps the doors would open which would lead me to that job or man or circumstances that would fulfill and complete me. I decided to leave Australia and return to America.

As *The Canberra* sailed past the Heads and slid out of Sydney Harbor in March of 1971, I *knew* without a doubt that I would return. Would I have stood on the deck so calmly, I wonder, had I had any inkling of the distractions, obstacles and detours which would postpone my desires and intentions for 20 years?

There would be a 13 year marriage to a dear, gentle man, whom I loved but with whom I was mismatched. There would be eight years of running my own flower business. There would be improved relations with my family and a move to

Oregon. And, there would be multiple sclerosis. With that, my life became a pattern of dropping one by one those things which I had once thought represented fulfillment--my marriage, my business, my body and my identity.

I embarked on an inward-bound journey--proceeding through a land of pain, dissolution and confusion. There was no map to follow and I had to become my own mentor. Just as when I hitchhiked across continents, I had to trust my intuition, had to trust my decisions about what were the right vehicles and the right directions for my progress.

The story of that journey is chronicled elsewhere.[1] I did survive, heal, and renew myself on every level: physically, emotionally and spiritually. And then my life became even fuller. In 1986 there appeared an exceptional man who was a reflection of this developing wholeness.

From the beginning of my life with Sid, I talked of Australia, of my dream of returning, and of my desire to share it all with him. Matching my eagerness, Sid helped keep the dream afloat and believed that one day we could make it happen. The dream came true, and this book is the fulfillment of my desire to share moments and places of our year *Down Under All Over.*

---

[1]   See the author's *Journey To Wholeness*. Published by Four Winds Publishing Co. 1991.

You can almost touch the ocean
Shimmering in the distant haze
As you stand there on the mountain
On this loveliest day of days

'Round half the world you've drifted
Left no wild oats unsown
But now your view has shifted
And you think you've just come home [1]

[1] from *Shelter* by Eric Bogle, and sung by John Williamson

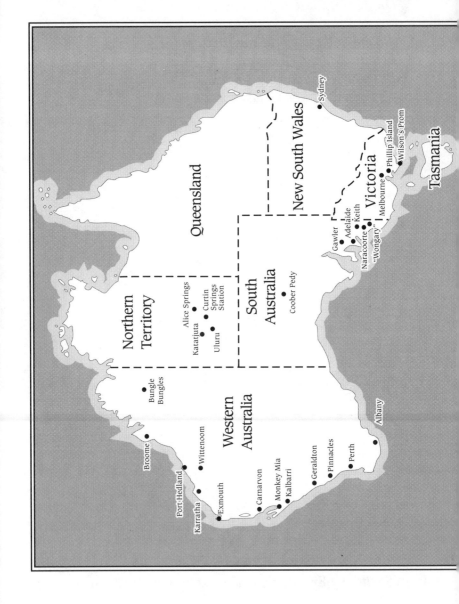

ARRIVAL

IT WAS FIVE-THIRTY in the morning as our jumbo jet approached Sydney. Australia, the focus of so much energy, so many visions, for so many years and days, was almost a reality. Under the weariness of the jagged, wrung-out night, excitement and anticipation smoldered within me, along with an overwhelming sense of homecoming. How often I'd dreamed of looking down on Sydney's Heads and the Harbor Bridge and crying. Now I sat on the wrong side of the plane and I was exhausted. Still I cried. The moment was big--it had been imagined and eluded me so long.

How could I be HERE? Here in this goal and dream of 20 years? While I felt profoundly awed, I was surprised to notice that being here seemed so easy and natural and had happened so fast that it was almost incomprehensible. Does the magic of jet travel deny us that sense of wonder in achieving distance and space?

When I immigrated and crossed the sea in 1967, my expectations increased with the days, building a huge momentum toward my arrival in Australia. Certainly the last three months before leaving the United States had been abuilding as well, with Sid and me planning and speculating and checking off the weeks. But it was not a physical momentum. It was images...done in one spot, carried out as we moved thoroughly immersed in the moments and the demands of the place we were in.

Flying to Sydney meant that instead of moving geographically closer, over days, we were crossing half the world in a matter of hours. The previous morning we'd dunked in Oregon's Sandy River, in the afternoon I'd rummaged for a last time amidst my shelves and books, and then had shared a late lunch with friends. Twenty-four hours later I would stand in the customs line at Sydney Airport, having entered a tubular room on one side of the world and emerged from it on the other.

Not that our time spent in the sky had not seemed interminable-- sitting in straight-backed seats, wedged narrowly between other passengers, no room for knees or for laying back in comfort. Our day of travel consisted of a two hour flight from Portland to San Francisco and a two hour wait. Five hours flying to Honolulu and

1

another delay. Then nearly ten hours in a giant jet on our final leg to Sydney. Even so, it was too quick, too expansive to comprehend; but not something to be denied or wished away. My perceptions of the world changed as I changed.

Three years earlier when Sid and I first rented out our house and began our vagabond life together, we had expected a quick realization of our Australian dream. But doors had opened in other wonderful directions and it had been appropriate to go through them. Now, at last, my intention to return was finally coming to fruition. To what purpose? For when and what? How? Where? What did I bring to this country that I'd remembered and yearned after for twenty years? A new wholeness, a sense of giving rather than taking, a desire to offer whatever gifts had grown within me, gifts which I myself didn't as yet understand and wasn't sure of the form they might take. And Sid--how would he respond to a country he'd never been to before?

It was impossible to foresee how the year would evolve. Our "plan" was to visit the Pereys in Perth in Western Australia and then to see other friends in the East. In order to crisscross the country on our terms and in comfort, we would probably buy a car. Beyond that, we would let the country and our budget direct our course. We would be looking for opportunities to help out on stations,* farms and youth hostels--any place where we could participate in daily activities. Even the length of our stay was uncertain. Although our airline tickets were good for a year, our visas were good for only six months, and we had no way of knowing whether or not we'd be granted an extension.

Dear friends waited to see us--new friends waited to be made. We were not "transiting to Melbourne," as were most of our fellow passengers. Had that been the case, we would soon have been enveloped in warm welcomes and long awaited reunions with my friends in the eastern states. Instead, we were going to Perth to be with Katherine and Nick first. Thanks to the nationwide airline strike, however, that much-anticipated reunion was postponed. We were destined to layover in Sydney.

So we might as well accept the unexpected detour. Once we'd suspended the panicky litany of "I have to get to Perth," we relaxed. We could even be happy with the situation, instead of joining hoards of harried folks frantic to get somewhere they were not. Landing in unknown circumstances, with no idea where we would go or what would happen, with no old friendships to rely on, Sid and I embarked on a new way of life together--and a new adventure.

SYDNEY TWENTY YEARS LATER

SYDNEY IN SEPTEMBER was spring sun leaning out of a pale sky against which the new green of jacarandas and silk trees formed frail patterns. It was cool, long shadows stealing along warm brick walls and old fashioned streets. And it was rising from Robert's lounge room* floor to the hum of morning traffic and the clattering of trains running through nearby New Town Station.

Sydney was also a delay and a bonus. On the one hand, we were disappointed to be halted on the brink of my much anticipated reunion with Perth and with my dear friends, Katherine and Nick Perey. On the other hand, the pilot strike gave us an opportunity to visit Sydney.

When I rang Katherine to explain our thwarted progress, she insisted that we call her son, Robert, who lived in Sydney. She, too, would give him a ring, and she was sure he'd offer to put us up.

I'd met Robert when he was barely a teenager. I was living in Perth in 1969 and was discovering that special friendship and wisdom of Katherine's which would inspire and guide me over miles and years to come. Her strength, determination and willingness to explore and employ all possibilities in her battle with cancer had taught and inspired me even before I faced multiple sclerosis and embarked on my own journey of healing. And it was thanks to Katherine's urgings that I'd started writing about my experience of MS and about my process of healing and self-discovery. We had much to share, and it was a lesson in utmost patience to put Perth, Katherine, my anticipations and desires aside and focus on Sydney and the present.

In his nonchalant way, Robert rose to his mother's offer, giving us the privacy of his small, square, but tall-ceilinged lounge room, two floor mats and a huge comforter to warm us in the cold and drafty terrace house. The building was similar to the one I'd lived in when I was in Perth, though not nearly so well maintained. Outside, the characteristic wrought iron balustrade on the second story hung askew, and freckled white paint peeled from the front facade. As with most of the other terrace houses which formed rows along each

4

side of the street, a miniscule patch of overgrown tropical creepers and weeds tangled between the house and a stucco and iron entry fence.

Indoors, air rushed in between window and door frames. The lights to the loo* at the end of the narrow back yard didn't work. The shower shed tacked on to the kitchen sported a sky view through gaping ceiling holes and discouraged any show of modesty thanks to a door incapable of shutting. Because of breaking and entering problems, Robert was in no hurry to upgrade the house. He kept the window shades pulled, so the interior remained dank and dark even on sunny days. I was thankful for Robert's hospitality *and* glad to be visiting in spring rather than winter. Despite such drawbacks, terrace houses were all the rage and were worth a good deal.

It was impossible to predict how soon we could expect a flight to Perth, which remained the most difficult of all Australian cities to reach. The pilots' strike continued to shut down the entire country. The only flights available were with international carriers and, unlike Melbourne and other major cities, Perth was not serviced by many of them. Each day we paid our respects to Ansett Airlines or Qantas only to learn that flights were still unavailable. With that chore behind us, we then sallied forth to enjoy our bonus time in Sydney--compliments of the pilots.

Enmore, the rather run down, but delightfully ethnic suburb where Robert's house was located, was a twenty minute train ride from downtown Sydney. Each day Sid and I walked to the train station, assailed by the exotic fragrances, colors, and wares in the rows of old-fashioned, dingy, local shops. Every nationality seemed to be represented. There were Lebanese bakeries, Greek, Vietnamese, and Italian groceries and delis. Colorful vegetables and flowers lined little greengrocers' shops. There was even a Mexican restaurant--something totally unheard of in Australia in the sixties.

We couldn't walk through this daily feast of exotic smells and bright colors without sampling some new treat or other. Then we'd descend the stone stairway to the New Town Station platform and await the train in the cool morning sun. On Robert's recommendation, we'd each bought a $13 Red Pass, which was good for a week and allowed us unlimited use of the trains, busses and ferries.

What I most noticed about Sydney twenty years later was the rundown look--not downtown or in the upscale neighborhoods--but in certain surrounding suburbs. Vandalism and marring of public property in these areas was very evident. The trains, especially, were unattractive. Trains as well as stations had had all advertising posters removed, and in their empty spots peeled green paint covered with black graffiti scribbles. Damaged seats were ill-repaired with ugly yellow and brown-plaid cheap vinyl. Some cushions bulged with exposed stuffing. Signs on the walls cautioned: THIS TRAIN PATROLLED BY PLAINCLOTHES AND UNIFORMED POLICEMEN ....NO SMOKING...$2OO FEE FOR VANDALIZING. Toilets in the stations carried signs proclaiming: THESE RESTROOMS CLOSED IN ORDER TO MAINTAIN PUBLIC SAFETY. Urine smells raged from outside the men's area. Benches drooped broken and discolored. Graffiti patterned walls, pavements and tunnels. Passengers looked grim.

But there were some changes that were delightful. Twenty years ago in Sydney dark faces had been conspicuous for their absence. Now the once white facial landscape displayed a fascinating blend of browns, blacks, yellows and whites. The food landscape, too, had taken on a rich new texture. Although standard restaurant meals seemed expensive (about $8 for lunch), we were able to sample (for reasonable prices) a delightful variety of international flavors--Lebanese, Greek, Indian, Thai, Vietnamese--available from the little take-out lunch bars which flourished everywhere

Twenty years earlier such food was found in the ethnic sections of the city only, and you didn't see Australians eating it. It was a rare Aussie who considered food horizons beyond a chop, a roast or a steak, and the not-so-fast, take-out food of the time was fish and chips. All that has changed with the influx of a new population. Now, we saw gyros, kabobs, spring rolls, and the ubiquitous McDonalds burgers gripped in contented Aussie hands.

Each day Sid and I handled business details such as searching for transformers, adaptors and cords to run our computer and printer. We opened bank accounts and exchanged money--which was fun because $100 US would swell to $120 Australian and we'd leave the bank feeling like we'd just hit the jackpot. Quite the opposite from 1967 when every $100 US dwindled to $88 Australian. Sid and I were also pleased to learn that regular bank accounts were earning interest rates of 13 to 14 and 15 to 16 percent.

Sydney's style was still as I remembered it, a charmingly cluttered combination of flavors. There were ponderous, dark eighteenth century buildings overshot by soaring glass sky scrapers; some streets were as wide and angular as others were windy and narrow. Buildings with tall, European-narrow fronts and many-chimneyed tile rooftops clustered on hillsides ribboned with zig zagging stairways or narrow alleys. Sydney combined the sleekness of America with the old world quaintness of Europe, heavily spiced with the almost Caribbean flavor of heavy grillwork verandas, cobblestone streets, palm trees and luxuriant green parks.

We strolled the elegant paths of the Royal Botanic Gardens, which were lined with the magnificent drapery-like trunks and dark green foliage of stately Morton Bay figs. In 1967, a friend from *The Himalaya* and I clambered over the locked gates and out again taking a shortcut to a restaurant. Now with Sid, sedately and with leisure, I enjoyed the bright-faced daffodils, colorful azaleas and exotic orchids displayed in blue and white marquees pitched on the well-groomed lawns. Each day was spring-warm and the benches and lawns were sprinkled with people reading papers, snacking, minding children or watching the play of water birds.

In the Domain, a nearby open stretch of grassland, we jogged out to "Mrs. Macquarie's Point." I decided I'd have liked Mrs. Macquarie. A sign explained: "Because she loved to sit here and enjoy the view, her husband, an early Governor of the colony, had a "chair" carved into the stone hillside."

In the rosy glow of sundown, we rode the stocky little ferries, watching as crowds of commuters disembarked at quaint little ramps and piers strewn along the length of the harbor. We walked the bustling downtown streets where some buildings maintain the original Victorian interiors of black and white tiles, polished dark woods, ornate filigrees and curlicues. As we followed our city map, we became acquainted with an Aussie custom which would plague us on city corners as well as in the remote crossroads of the outback. When arriving at certain intersections, we'd be left frustratingly ignorant of our location because of the Australian habit of omitting signposts.

On the waterfront not far from the Harbor Bridge, we walked the flagstone terraces of the famous Sydney Opera House. Twenty years before it had been regarded as either Australia's greatest claim to fame or as the country's biggest boondoggle. After many years and countless cost increases (from $12 million to over $100 million), the ambitious project was still under construction in 1967, but the structure's white-swept wings already dominated Bennelong Point. Now, walking at last beneath the billowing sails of the completed Opera House, enjoying the fresh breezes off the indigo water, Sid and I hugged each other and for the umpteenth time that day, said, "I can't believe we're really here."

No matter where we were, I always related my location back to the Harbor Bridge--dubbed by locals, "The Coat Hanger." Its span for me had always been Sydney's focal point. In 1967 *The Himalaya* had docked in Sydney Cove with the mighty bridge looming high and dark astern of us. On that first Australian evening, I walked across the bridge. The setting sun had hung suspended like a red ball, diffusing a rosy glow over the entire western horizon of the city. In my exuberance, I broke into a run, laughing and singing. Stopping in the middle of the bridge, I mentally hugged myself, wondering at the wonder of it all. The Harbor Bridge! I thought it beautiful--like the country--not delicate at all. Rather it was a powerful, imposing, self-asserting structure--ambitious--just like the country. The bridge symbolized Sydney and Australia, and all my dreams, and I felt that the country was waiting, ready to offer up infinite possibilities if I cared to take them.

Sid and I loved each day's exploration. But I found it surprising that I did not feel wrapped up in the place. Being in Sydney was not enough. The key for me was in how I related to the people. I'd yet to see Katherine and my other friends...or the new ones I was to meet. Nor was Sydney the Australian countryside--the small towns--that so attracted me. Being in Sydney was indeed an achievement; after twenty years and countless delays, I was at last on Australian soil. But I realized it wasn't Sydney or the cities that had pulled me. It was the people and the land that called and I was not yet there.

PERTH

AFTER FIVE DAYS in Sydney, Sid and I finally managed to get on a flight to Perth. Delighted, we went on our way to the airport--only to run smack into a sixteen-hour delay. Not until three o'clock in the morning did we exhaustedly set foot in the Perth air terminal. Despite the hour, Katherine and Nick were there, Katherine beaming and flying toward me with outstretched arms. At their home, after snatches of chatter and cups of herb tea, we were ushered into our flower-filled room, welcome sign on the door, and collapsed into bed.

Katherine and Nick were among the many Europeans who found a new life in Australia after World War II. Nick, tall and aristocratic looking, but down-to-earth with a sweet sense of humor, had been an officer in the Hungarian army. He found a job driving busses with the Perth bus system and remained with the company until he retired several years ago.

Katherine, so petite when standing beside her tall husband, looked wonderfully fit and happy. Her bright blue eyes constantly twinkled. As she talked animatedly in her lilting German accent, her words often tumbled so fast that she grabbed at German words in place of the English ones which did not come fast enough to keep up with her rapid thought processes. She was as intense and involved in diverse activities as always, and Sid and I quickly found ourselves included in many of them, such as the Unity church, rebirthing, silent retreats, a meditation group, counseling, the Course in Miracles, tennis, grandchildren and friends, etc.

Every day someone dropped in to visit--often staying late into the night. Once a fortnight*, as they had done for the last thirty years, Katherine and Nick rose at four o'clock in the morning to go to the growers' market. There they purchased a trailer load of produce for distribution to eighteen families. For their efforts Katherine and Nick received their vegetables free. Once they returned home, a steady stream of people converged on their place. More than vegetables were exchanged, though, as many people stayed to talk long and earnestly with Katherine, whose wisdom, guidance and

9

intuition were sought by friends and strangers alike.

   We had fun visiting Katherine and Nick's son, Rolf, who with his wife, Mim, lived in the spring-green hills of Perth. Rolf and Mim had visited me in Portland years ago. They'd been in their early twenties then but had already mastered the art of being guests-- eagerly digging and weeding in my garden, cooking up quiche dinners, and taking themselves out of the house frequently enough so that I still had my privacy. Now in their thirties, they still displayed that same artistry in their approach to life. Rolf had left the teaching profession and established himself as a photographer. They and their darling baby son lived in a classic country house which they were remodeling and re-facing brick by scrounged brick. Freesias, azaleas and wild bulbs bloomed like a carpet throughout the sprawling yard. Chooks* and cats perched on the porches that completely wrapped around the house. And Rolf and Mim took long walks and tea breaks and left for month-long camping trips--thus keeping themselves fresh and the whole thing in perspective.

   One day we all went to visit Matthew, an old friend of mine. In 1969 Matthew had been part of Perth's artistic crowd that frequented The Pink Pig where I was a wine waitress. Matthew had been an aspiring and rebellious film maker with a fascinating and volatile personality, and he and I spent several months dancing through a tender but confusing relationship. I think of that time as my Bohemian Period--characterized by poverty, wit, lingering late-night discussions over espresso and wine, Italian restaurants, galleries, opening nights and hobnobbing with Perth's small, but vital, artistic colony.

   Time had not been kind to Matthew. A thin, furrowed man wearing grubby, baggy jeans, a dirty red pullover and a big grin, he hailed us from his big backyard. His face was drawn and deeply etched with wrinkles, and his brow creased with intensity as he spoke. He still talked with the purpose of throwing people off balance and evaded giving direct answers. This man, who was at once a mix of intimate memories and a stranger, elicited in me feelings of sadness--sadness for his evasion and dishonesty, and for his rundown look and life--as if he simply couldn't find what was the right track for him. I still thought of him as a sweet man, but a loser, playing the rebel and taking a certain pride in his solitude and

10

poverty. He was stubbornly stuck in his "I'm going to do it my way" attitude. This had attracted me twenty years ago. Now, somehow, it struck me as solitary and sad. We parted with polite but empty noises about keeping in touch.

*　　　　*　　　　*

Rolf had kindly loaned us his ute*. Driving this mud-colored, rusty and time-creased vehicle was an unequaled travel experience. Usually I was hilariously laughing as Sid negotiated the left-side* driving with the indicator switch between his teeth, one hand repeatedly coaxing the gears to shift, the other hand steering, while the windswipes* clattered futilely and my door flew open every time we turned a corner. Once we parked the ute on a hill facing a brick wall. When we prepared to leave, the reverse shift wouldn't work. Fortunately Sid quickly figured out the problem, crawled under the car with his trusty belt pliers and tightened the wheezy old bolt.

Katherine and Nick's substantial brick house adjoined the lawns of a pretty city park containing rust colored concrete paths, a soccer field and tennis backboards. Just down the street stood the high school with "our" private tennis courts, and not far beyond was a public pool.

I enjoyed jogging along the streets of the old neighborhood of Mt. Lawley. Everything was done in rusts. Red brick houses sported either red tile or corrugated iron roofs. Fences were made of solid sheets of corrugated asbestos dyed russet from the local water, and which looked surprisingly attractive. Footpaths* and even the tree trunks were stained rust-red. As I jogged past the gardens filled with exotic palms, jacaranda and gum trees, I was continually assailed by the fragrance of citrus, stock, acacia, and the most profusely blooming rose bushes I'd ever seen.

There was an overhead danger in this placid scene. The magpies were nesting and were very protective of their young. Several times I nearly leaped out of my skin as heart-stopping squawks pierced the air, and a black and white missile repeatedly dived at my head. I quickly learned to walk wide of the trees. Newspapers cautioned parents to put hats on their children, and park strollers and joggers carried sticks.

11

The weather was Oregonish--grey, wet, cloudy, cold--everything we thought we'd left behind. Like most Aussie houses, Katherine and Nick's lacked a heating system. This didn't bother them, as they were hardy folks, who thrived on what to overheated Americans seemed like a meat locker temperature. It must have worked, too, because at seventy-plus both were energetic, active and well-preserved. Sid, who is warm blooded, sat down to dinner in his heaviest winter jacket. I sat swathed in borrowed wool sweaters, scarves and double layers of sox, wishing I could work the computer keyboard wearing mittens. At night I'd burrow into bed with a hot water bottle--which was literally a glass bottle--under layers of blankets, topping it off with a huge pink comforter so heavy that I'd wonder if I'd emerge in the morning several inches longer and flatter.

In 1969 Australians had been flocking to the West because of the mineral discoveries in the far north and the city of Perth was booming. Cranes overhung the entire city. Land Rovers clogged the main thoroughfares. In 1990 the streets of Perth were crammed with cars of all kinds. There were more roads and highways, and cranes still honeycombed the downtown area. Perth had grown a lot. As changes go, though, they were gratifying. Downtown streets were wide. Some had been turned into car-less malls. The small town, country flavor was retained in the bevy of small shops bordering the streets and the frontier-like covered porches which shaded many footpaths. The impression was of buildings, streets and sidewalks being light and clean. In contrast to Sydney, Perth looked rich. The busses and trains and the people riding them looked new and clean.

Perth had been an easy town to get around in twenty years ago. Whether I was heading downtown to my silk screen classes at the West Australian Institute of Technology, or going to an outer suburb, I only had to stand on the street with my thumb out. I always got a ride--usually right to the doorstep of my destination. Only rarely did I resort to using the trains. Now I noticed that the train station had been remodeled into a complex linking with the museum, Institute of Technology, and art galleries on one side of the tracks and a huge department store and terraced shopping center on the other. It was all glass and grids and tiles and sky and white bricks and fountains. Very impressive.

12

Subiaco, where I'd lived in 1969 and where The Pink Pig was located, had changed from a sleepy little suburb into a trendy, Yuppy-like community. Colorfully painted specialty shops and fancy complexes lined the busy streets. What I presumed to be Catherine Street (it lacked a street sign) where my terrace house had been, was now one-way only; and such houses, I was told, rented for top prices.

Around the corner, I was unable to recognize Mr. Smith's house. He was a dear old man whom I met when I was looking for a piano to play. I'd reconnoitered my neighborhood deciding which houses looked likely to contain pianos. My reckoning had been right. Within moments of knocking on Mr. Smith's door, I was ushered in to play the piano. Within the week he'd had it tuned, and from then on I established the habit of coming over to practice for a couple of hours each day. Mr. Smith loved to listen and always saw to it that I had cups of tea and plenty of his home-grown chocolate covered almonds.

The Pink Pig, alas, was no more. But The Hole In The Wall Theater still existed. There, in 1969 I made my Western Australian theater debut as a Golliwog*, a role which demanded little verbal finesse but a lot of running around.

Kings Park, a 1000 acre reserve, is to Perth what Golden Gate Park is to San Francisco. On a bright blue, sparkling spring day Sid and I walked every segment of the Botanic Gardens with their tropical plants and Victorian gazebos overlooking Perth and the wide Swan River. Royal rows of mighty eucalyptus lined the park's drives and walks, each tree bearing a plaque commemorating a dead soldier. Wild flowers were coming into full bloom and we strolled through fragrant fields of pink and white everlastings--flowers that I'd strived to grow for drying and for use in arrangements during my eight years in the flower business. We happened on a festival of pavilions displaying native wild flowers, many of them familiar because they've been imported to California. Others were so exotic as to boggle the eye with brilliant colors, odd textures and winged shapes.

In many ways Western Australia, and particularly Perth, are to Australia what California is to the United States. Easterners have increasingly migrated westward, just as Americans have done in the last twenty years. Perth and the surrounding suburbs exuded an atmosphere of bustling growth, positivism and pride, and a sense of wealth prevailed. I'd worried that the influx of money, ideas and commercialism from the Americas Cup event would ruin Perth. Indeed it changed Perth but not disastrously so.

The nearby town of Freemantle, even more so than Perth, had been altered by the infusion of Americas Cup money. Like a woman who's undergone a fashion make-over, Freemantle had come alive. What was once a dingy, dark-stoned, sleepy historical port, was now a sparkling, clean-lined, attractive town. That the brightly painted facades and sanded stones housed typical tourist T-shirt and post card shops couldn't be denied or criticized. It was still an attractive makeover.

During the October school holidays, another guest joined us at the Pereys. Sandra, a fourteen year old student at a girls' school, moved into Nick's office/bedroom in preference to returning to her far-away home in Brunei (near Malaysia) for the two-week break. We were beginning to realize that visitors were a way of life with Nick and Katherine. Sandra's father had once been one of the many people who had found his way to the house on Woodsome Street and stayed a while.

One day the five of us piled into our hosts' station wagon and drove to Serpentine--a hamlet about 45 minutes south of Perth--to visit their friend who was a monk in a Buddhist monastery. After parking inside the yellow brick and wrought iron entry gates, we learned that the friend was in the temple meditating as this was the week of their Rains Retreat. Disappointed at missing him, we set off to explore.

The monastery property was pretty and well groomed. The main building, the brick temple, was attractively designed. We strolled the shrubby grounds on well-defined crisscrossing trails. Occasionally we glimpsed monks wrapped in saffron robes and topped with stocking caps gliding swiftly through the shadowy bush.

To our delight we spotted a mother roo* and joey* sniffing at us a few meters down the hillside. Only after we turned to go on did they casually continue grazing and then hopping on their way.

I hung back from our group, wanting to savor the peaceful atmosphere and the deep silence of the bushy hillsides. Ever since arriving in Australia, I'd wanted to find that pervasive silence. It was difficult to achieve in my neighborhood walks and in the cities. I'd wanted the same connection I'd felt with the trees where we lived on the Sandy River in Oregon, and now here it was.

As sundown shadows darkened the blue green flagstones, the

monks emerged from the temple and we met Katherine and Nick's friend. He was vibrant, witty and chatty, and comfortable with breaking his silence to visit with us. Sid and I also talked with the abbot about our coming to stay for a few days. I was not so much interested in the formal Buddhist teachings as I was drawn to the atmosphere of devotions, discipline and right living. I liked these gentle men and their humor and their exemplary ways and I wanted to learn from them. On that day the seed of a new adventure was planted, and both Sid and I were determined that somehow we would return to the monastery.

As we drove home, I was struck by the extraordinary mixture Australia represented. Here were two Americans, a German, a Hungarian, and a Malay girl from Brunei, and we'd been talking with an Englishman who was a Buddhist monk in a monastery in Australia, founded and funded by Thais and run by an Italian abbot. I liked it.

Our first Aussie vehicle, the "ute."

THE ROYAL PERTH SHOW

IT WAS SPRING in Perth, and Sid and I took in the Royal Show--sort of a big town country fair. What a great way for foreigners to get a glimpse of the country. There were the typical agricultural, horticultural, and industrial pavilions--well-presented, but delightfully unslick and unsophisticated. There were booths where microphoned barkers demonstrated chamois and peelers and gadgets. There were bakery booths, water board booths, tourism booths and a lovely Men of the Trees booth where I bought several 5 cents stickers with zany slogans like "Roos get jaded if not shaded," "Save your ranches, plant some branches," and "Trees are the bee's knees."

We enjoyed most the central Oval events. First were the sheep dog trials--a stunning and beautiful display of the intelligence, patience and cleverness of these marvelous dogs. Each dog had to maneuver three sheep about the wide oval lawn area, around selected pegs, into two separate chutes, and finally into a pen, always keeping the sheep to the right shoulder of the trainer who directed the dog and walked ahead of him to each new section of the course.

Next we were fascinated by the "Cavalcade of Tractors"--an incredible assortment of steaming and chortling antique tractors driven by pink cheeked country chaps, shy and proud in their moment of glory.

Then came the grand parade, a kind of Noah's Ark of farm animals and people. Children filed round the grassy Oval tethered to goats, calves, or tank sized cows. Groups of horsemen on magnificent blooded stock danced past the grandstand identified as to their breed by signs stating: "Warm Bloods," "Cold Bloods," "White Horse Breeds," "Caspians" and others. Princely ponies pranced beneath correctly clad youngsters. A certain cleanliness and formality prevailed which I found quite appealing. Most riders were neatly outfitted in English riding attire and many of those leading the animals wore white lab coats. No one was dressed in dirty, torn or baggy clothes.

The conglomeration of animals and people paraded past in crisscrosses of cavorting colors, sizes, shapes. These people, little and big, were so INVOLVED, so obviously taking pleasure in the moment and in their animals. There was an innocence and appeal that touched me so deeply that tears ran down my face.

Leaving the Oval we walked the noisy, crowded grounds smelling the pungent odors of straw and manure mingling with the savory aroma of sizzling sausages, roast mutton and frying onions. Everyone in the milling crowd of children and adults seemed to be eating something--pink, wispy fairy floss*, lamb shanks on white bread, ice cream cones, icy poles*, sausage rolls, and cream-filled waffle roll-ups to name a few.

Our steps took us through the densely crowded carnival section where music blared and machinery whirled ferris wheels and other thrilling rides in a whiz of bright blurring colors. We just missed the log chopping contest and I was disappointed to find the cat, rabbit and cavy* pavilions deserted. The judging for those animals was done and they'd all gone home. I'd been very curious about the cavies, particularly about an event titled Cavy Races. (Pronounced cave-y) If you can guess what a cavy is you are sharper than I was. I had to ask!

At the bird exhibits we saw rows and rows of fantastic fantailed pigeons whose tail feathers spread out in gorgeous arrays of grays, greens and teal blues. We also saw something I'd never heard of, let alone seen--"Silky Chickens." Their white feathers were as fluffy as if they were cat fur. The chickens sort of made up for missing the cats.

As we drove home Sid and I chattered and chuckled about the discoveries and experiences of that delightful day. The memories would glow for a long time to come.

"AUSSIE-ISMS"

IT'S A PLACE where animals have names like wallabies, wombats and bandicoots--and where lyrebirds and platypuses (platypusies? platypie?) abide. To me, the fairytale names on Australian maps, roadsigns, suburbs and letterheads contrast oddly with the population of British background culture they support. The people who casually call "home" names like Wagga Wagga, Widgemultha, Tarra Bulga, Korumburra, Jaramanjumup...are the same people who have "Tidy Town" contests, break for tea two or three times a day, and consider "coffee" to be an instant powder.

Some of the Australian customs appeared to be very British in their consideration for comfort and neatness. Beaches, for example, consistently provided frequent and free shower facilities for bathers. Where, in certain European countries, it seems the only public facilities evident are for men and, where in the States, I might have to search out a department store or service station in order to use a toilet, in Australia such facilities were liberally sprinkled throughout cities, suburbs, and even the smallest towns. Not only were they available, but they were not hidden. Easily discerned blue and white " Toilets" signs dotted buildings and street corners, pointing you in the correct direction.

Certain differences in terminology could be confusing as well as entertaining. For example, in the States I might ask for the rest room and expect to be directed to a room with a toilet. In Australia a rest room comprised much more. In nearly every country town the omnipresent CWA, (Country Women's Association) provided an often large facility titled the Ladies Rest Room. Besides toilets and washbasins, rest rooms typically contained showers, baby changing area, sometimes even ironing boards and refrigerators. It was a wonderful offering for women coming into town from outlying properties who might need such various forms of "rest".

Not unusually, country road houses (service stations) and city department stores also offered such conveniences. Typical again, of the way women's needs were looked after, in some department stores were counters labeled "Parcel Check Desk" so that a lady need not cart her packages into the toilet.

The ubiquitous Women's Restroom.

Which brings me to toilets. When Australians speak of the toilet, they are referring to a room, not to the commodity in it. I was shocked when a little girl told me, "When our cat had kittens, we kept them in the toilet." The "bathroom" is literally that, and nothing more. If I were in a department store and asked, "Could you direct me to the bathroom?" the clerks looked amused. "Silly Yank," they must have thought, "Fancy wanting a bath in a department store."

Other terms require translation. Tea for example is "tea" only if it is "morning tea" or "afternoon tea." If someone invites you over for tea, they are inviting you for the evening meal--what Americans call dinner. If an advertisement for an event says "Supper will be served," it means "refreshments" will be served, not dinner--although a country supper could so fill you up that you might wish

19

you hadn't eaten any tea. I noticed that in the last twenty years the use of the term tea, meaning dinner, had fallen off. As more Australians watched American TV, they had shifted over to using the American terms.

Other terms, too, had fallen by the wayside. Young Australians used to use the word "beaut" in the way young Americans used "neat." "It's a beaut dye (day)...He's a beaut bloke..." After some time in Australia, I'd only heard beaut used once. In America, "reckon," a word associated with cowboys and old time westerns, is rarely encountered. In Australia you run across it frequently, mostly used by country or labor-oriented folks.

Because breaking for a cup of something is so universal, the Aussies shorten the question to "Do yer want a cuppa?" If you ask for a cuppa coffee even in restaurants you get a beverage made from instant powder. If you don't distinguish black or white "coffee," it will always come white. In fact, Sid always asked for "coffee" black and it still arrived white.

A restaurant is a place where exorbitant prices are charged for miniscule servings of dismal attempts at gourmet food that never quite come off. A take-out shop can vary from one end of the scale to the other. In it are served reasonably priced sandwiches, fish and chips, burgers or other simple food which can be either dry, greasy and tasteless or marvelously delicious.

Bakeries are places where you see the same cream-filled donuts, flat custard slices, and lamingtons (square slices of sponge cake dipped in runny chocolate icing and rolled in coconut--an Aussie institution) as you've seen in every other bakery along the street or throughout the state. Once in a while a bakery will surprise you and produce some individual concoctions, but on the whole the offerings appear to have sprung from the same central mold, or out of some universal British recipe book.

One term that was never heard twenty years ago and which is now ubiquitous, is "kilometers." It was quite amazing to realize that an entire nation has seemingly overnight swept away the old method of measurements and completely adjusted to a new one. In a country where the distances are so vast, it seems rather contrary to speak in such small measurements as kilometers instead of miles. From what I saw, except in the outback, no one regrets or resists the change or hankers after the old ways. Even old timers talk in terms of kilometers--or "kays"--and kilograms, instead of miles and pounds. Evidently the government removed all the road signs, changed all the maps and texts and stationery, and everybody simply shifted. For a time it was actually illegal to sell rulers, etcetera, that were non-metric. Once the change was made, they became legal again.

By comparison, how silly and doomed-to-failure seem America's half-hearted attempts to change to metric. Putting up road signs in both metric and miles cancels any motivation to learn the new way. In Australia there is no alternative but to read, interpret, and organize distances in terms of kilometers, because that's all that's presented--although I, for one, continued to convert everything back to miles.

If your baby whinges (cries and complains), it could be because he has a wog (virus) and feels crook (ill). If you ask your husband to nurse the baby, he won't be shocked because he is only expected to hold it. Babies wear napkins, or nappies, instead of diapers, but you needn't worry when you sit down to tea (dinner), because you'll not be handed a napkin but a serviette.

I enjoy the differences in idiom. It was fun learning to speak in Aussie terms and to see through Aussie eyes, even though there were times when I might stare blankly at an Aussie, not understanding what was said or what was meant. Fortunately there was a constantly used Aussie term that covered such moments, in fact, *most* moments, and which expresses volumes about the Australian character: NO WORRIES. "Sorry, I didn't catch what you said." NO WORRIES, mate. "Thanks for the lovely tea." NO WORRIES. "The strike seems to be taking the country downhill." NO WORRIES. "Shall we eat breaky (breakfast) in that picnic spot?" NO WORRIES." There's nothing more to add to this article so I guess I'll throw my bathers (swimsuit) in the car boot (trunk) and head for the beach." NO WORRIES.

THE WEST COAST

WHILE IN PERTH Sid and I had hoped that some opportunity would present itself whereby we could house sit or stay rent-free in exchange for helping out with maintenance. The only glimmer of a possibility was a vague suggestion by friends of friends that a house might be available down in Albany in the south. But that wouldn't happen until December. After a month with Nick and Katherine, and after purchasing a car--a Holden Commodore--Sid and I left Perth.

We had no definite destination in mind except that we hoped to forge as far north as Broome, a place I had enjoyed twenty years ago and which I wanted to share with Sid. I felt slightly apprehensive, though, for I learned that Broome was now highly touted as a popular tropical resort. We also took the chance of running into very hot temperatures or The Wet*--either of which could influence and alter our course once we arrived in the North.

In a flurry of goodbyes and hugs, we left Nick and Katherine. Our car was laden with their borrowed sleeping bags, utensils and camping gear, and our esky* overflowed with offerings of Katherine's homemade bread and fresh market produce.

Our first stop, about three hours north of Perth, was the Pinnacles. They seemed to be a well-kept secret since they were not listed on the road map as Pinnacles. Instead, they were referred to as Nambung National Park--a name which offered no clues as to what one would find there. It was only because of Katherine and Nick's urgings, that we knew of the Pinnacles at all.

After driving for 11 km along a red dirt road flanked for miles by the repetitious grey-green scrub, road and scrub gave way to a yellow terrain. Yellow hard-packed sand dunes swept across several hillsides out of which rose a forest of weathered sandstone cones, looming like mute soldiers in a lunar landscape. The cones were in all sizes--from miniscule shapes to towering heights. Surprisingly appealing was the fact that cars were allowed to drive through the area. Small stones defined the yellow track and turnout points. We felt like characters in a fantasy as we sat in comfort, crawling along amidst that surrealistic setting, periodically stopping to get out and walk. It was a golden sunset hour and only one other car threaded between the streaking shadows of that stark and strange expanse.

Experts speculate that the Pinnacles are either the remains of a fossilized forest, or they could be a simple case of erosion. Whatever their origin, the Pinnacles are eloquent examples of the work of the elements, especially the wind. They were our introduction to the omnipresent west coast wind. It was a ceaseless driving force that maddeningly switched directions just after you finally found a perfect windbreak. It accompanied our coastal progress, and the locals said it was a constant factor in their lives. At least the wind was a blessing in that it kept things cool, kept the flies away, and was a strong excuse to avoid setting up our borrowed tent.

That night, in the nearby hamlet of Cervantes, we discovered the Australian custom of hiring caravans.* We found these to be roomy, comfortable, well-equipped, and inexpensive. In fact, a night's lodging for two in a caravan park could be cheaper than a stay at a youth hostel--from about $18 to $28 a night for the two of us. If we committed to staying a week, the price could be as low as $18.00 a night. The rule was always BYO (Bring Your Own) bedding. That first night in our hired caravan, we both beamed like children who had discovered a wonderful secret. We were snug and warm and out of the wind. We had a fridge in which to refreeze our water jugs for our esky and a stove for cooking. All utensils and even detergent and brillo pads were provided. Showers and toilets and laundry were mere steps away. And the glistening beach waited just down the slope.

The next day after a leisurely morning at Cervantes, we set out for Geraldton, the windy "Gateway to the Northwest." Some 425 km north of Perth, and the base for Western Australia's rock lobster industry, Geraldton seemed much bigger and newer than I remembered it. A bustling port, it had a big, bright Target store and neon-clad surfing lads lounging along the one main street bordering on a turquoise harbor. For $8 a night each, the youth hostel gave us a barren cubicle with a double bed on the enclosed front veranda. To reach the outdoor loo* we had first to walk into the house and then out again across the back yard.

I enjoyed visiting with the "youth" in the community kitchen, notwithstanding the fact that I felt slightly odd being in this setting with a car, computer and handsome husband. Like these youngsters, I'd relished the challenge of living on no money way back when. It was a fun game to foster my creativity by staying in back yards or parks, police stations or youth hostels, and hitching rides. One girl told me she'd caught a cab from the bus station to the hostel. It had never occurred to me in earlier days to make it that simple. Now I could say that I admired her style. These hostelers were larking along, staying a day or ten, depending on their mood. Sid and I related to them, but it seemed slightly incongruous, although very rewarding, to be larking at such a different level of means.

Sid and I had been urged to divert from the main north road so as to visit Kalbarri which was famous for its beaches and nearby red rock gorges. Our friends told us that it would be worth the extra 80 km. The next day, three hours north of Geraldton, we arrived in Kalbarri, a sleepy little hamlet at this pre-holiday time of year.

Once again I was grateful for the funds that allowed me to so easily opt for comfortable caravans and snug rooms rather than toughing it out in our borrowed tent. Not that I wouldn't have enjoyed perching on the bank overlooking Kalbarri's mighty Murchison River. I'd have liked stirring my spaghetti over our borrowed gas stove in the orange glow of the setting sun. But there was the wind! Wind and WIND! As we approached the historic hamlet of Greenough the previous day, we had seen gum trees growing parallel to the ground.

At night the wind wound down and stillness blossomed. Overhead, brilliant stars ignited a velvet sky. Then with the day, the wind revived, whipping white spray from breakers' crests, spitting splinters of sand against walking legs and sending beach goers in a vain search for sheltered spots.

On our first Kalbarri morning, I was up and into the computer first thing. Then we walked to town, or rather down the empty street that made up the town, in the calmest wind of the day. At long last we draped ourselves on our first Australian beach. Certainly it was beautiful. If our U. S. friends were to see a picture of this tropical scene, they would say, "Such a paradise." But they wouldn't know the true picture because the wind was not in view.

It was a pretty little bay, flanked by barren slips of hills. The muddy Murchison River curved in a gentle curlycue around a tiny sand bar, unfurling first into the turquoise waters of the bay, and then into the chomping breakers of the reef and the indigo ocean beyond. Dipping into the water was pleasant but not worth the wind chill that waited once out. Back in our caravan park we found the calmest spot against a wall by the swimming pool and sat down to read and swim.

Later we drove down to Red Bluff where the road ended 4 km south of Kalbarri. We encountered another beautiful white beach, but this time it curved into a huge wall of red rock sprawling like sloping plates into the ocean. Despite the furious wind, we were quite warm. In some spots we actually were protected and basked in the glowing beauty of immense rock walls the color of dried blood.

Above the vast slopes of red stone rose a pyramidal yellow hill. At its base was a small plateau where crumbled rock pieces had fallen to a jumbled rest. Rocks had broken away from the high hill in straight edged chunks--like the fallen pillars of ancient temples. One enormous house-sized square perched so perfectly smooth-sided as if it had been cut to some mythical specifications.

As we walked beneath the rising yellow walls, I felt as if I had happened upon some sacred spot--like an ancient temple grounds. Further on, the square smooth stone turned rough, once again hewn into contorted shapes by erosion. Overhead, the yellow rim jutted like a row of crocodile snouts against the brilliant blue sky.

We were both unwinding and enjoying the peaceful private time. I began to accept the fact that I was on a holiday. Before leaving Perth, I'd been intent on interacting with people whom I could help and guide and serve--friends with problems, hospice patients-- anyone. I saw that as my offering and my gift and therefore my purpose in being anywhere. I couldn't accept that I could simply vacation, simply sit on a beach, ride in a car or camp in a caravan and not be serving and sharing. I'd felt reluctance about our trip north, wondering what I was here for and what was it leading me to?

Only on that day in Kalbarri, did I fully accept that I was there for *now*, not for some future goal. I was being handed a holiday. I was in the country I'd dreamed of, and I was healthy, loved, and had everything I needed. Yet I had been resisting and questioning the purpose of this journey just as I had questioned the journey through illness that began six years before. In that time of difficulty I'd

25

constantly clung to the awareness that I was learning to trust and that all the confusions would make sense in retrospect. That turned out to be true. Looking back, I'd finally recognized the gifts of those years and how as certain parts of me broke down, other unknown parts surfaced and developed.

How odd it was then, that even during the pleasant times of our journey north, I felt doubtful and confused about where it was all leading, felt unable to accept the present for the perfection it was. I still wanted the universe to put up billboards. I still longed for clarity of direction. I was *still* learning that life is limbo and the direction essentially vague. What I should also have known, having come through the hard passages, was that it was all right. I was in Kalbarri for--*Whatever.* I didn't have to *know* what for. I realized that I *can*, though, enjoy the process. Since it had taken the shape of a holiday, then, by gum, I would holiday!

The beach was white and warm, if windy. My body loved the sun and air. I could read, I could swim in the caravan park pool, walk and tour with Sid, eat bakery treats and succulent fresh fish and crisp chips--Ah! A holiday. A gift! Enjoy!

THE DOLPHINS OF MONKEY MIA

WE CAME TO Monkey Mia, I with much anticipation. What would I feel seeing wild dolphins right next to me? I knew I'd be greatly moved. And I was. Moved by their innocence and beauty and grace, and for the gift they give to us humans by choosing to venture into our waiting circle.

Ten hours north of Perth, and 25 wind-driven kilometers across from Denham on the Peron Peninsula, on a sealed* road no less, we turned into the red dirt parking lot of Monkey Mia. I was pleased to find a ranger and signs and brochures telling us HOW TO MEET THE DOLPHINS: Don't touch the blow hole. Pet them on their side. If a dolphin gives you a fish, accept it gratefully, don't give it back, etc.

In the attractive new ranger building overlooking the beach, we learned more from a well-done presentation. History is replete with instances of dolphins befriending mankind, but nowhere else in the world today do a number of dolphins make regular contact with humans. The puzzling name of Monkey Mia may have derived from the fact that Chinese once worked in the pearling industry there and were known as monkeys, while Mia is an aboriginal word for abode. Another speculation is that monkeys once were found locally.

Stepping off the red packed dirt parking area, we stood on a wide white beach commanding a vista of a turquoise bay. Groups of people were scattered along the beach, some reading books, some chatting, many looking expectantly at the water. It was a patient group, quiet, almost subdued as if awaiting a holy event. No one knew when the dolphins would come, or if they would appear at all. A pair of dolphins had already shown up earlier that morning. We were told that they were especially predictable during the summer months and had been so since the 1940's. What attracts them to this particular place and this contact with man? No one really knows.

Sid and I sat on our towels reading and sunning like the other waiters. An hour--perhaps two--passed. The breeze was brisk, though not too cold. The sun was warm and the sky, sea and beach were as pristine and inviting as a virgin tropical island.

Suddenly we were aware of people crowding in the water off to our left. A dolphin swam just in front of them. We hurried to join the group that was standing hushed and smiling and clacking cameras in the presence of this phenomenon.

I managed a brief slide of my hand along the dolphin's slippery body. He was gliding two to three feet away--just enough out of reach to make it inappropriate to lunge out to touch him. Mostly I stood knee deep in the clear water, along with the 30 or so others, waiting for a chance to snap a shot, or to pet him, all the while silently communing to the dolphin: "Thank you. I honor you and the gift of your presence."

Out of the turquoise waters, a second silver flash appeared arcing smoothly toward us. It, too, glided along our waiting ranks, lolling

The Dolphins of Monkey Mia.

sideways, much the way a cat tips belly-up, displaying its vulnerability and hence its trust. The dolphins seemed to be smiling up at us.

A young lady ranger wearing hip boots stood in the water directing the crowd to stand back, cautioning us not to put our hands on the dolphins' heads--which is their sensitive sensory area. They let us know they didn't like being touched there by quickly rearing backwards and thwacking the water.

Another ranger appeared with fish hidden in plastic bags inside his jacket. Already the giant pelicans, who earlier were dozing or strutting among the beach people, were furiously paddling around the dolphins, ready to dive for the fish. It became quite a tempestuous scene, the ranger driving back the ardent lumbering pelicans as well as some very cheeky cormorants. Three or four fish were handed to watchers to feed the dolphins, who gracefully seized the fish and glided away.

Several times the dolphins disappeared into the deeper waters only to return again. After an hour's visit, though, they apparently decided it was time to return from whence they'd come. We, the watchers, continued to stand gazing into the distance, as if reluctant to release the experience of that incredible past hour.

I felt a loss as the two silver shadows disappeared, returning to a watery world where they were at home and where we couldn't follow. The loss, too, was of these gentle creatures who harbored some special wisdom that urged them to leave their domain and to associate with the world of men.

The dolphins take the initiative. It is their choice to come to Monkey Mia. What is their message? What do they teach us? To respect and honor all creatures, one for the other. In that unique place it is man that does the responding, and I was pleased by what I saw. Monkey Mia was not commercialized and sensationalized. Great care had been taken to respect the dolphins and to instill a sense of wonder in those who come to see them. The special quality of Monkey Mia is summed up by Wilf Mason, the local "grandfather of the dolphins". In a world of seeming darkness, says Wilf, Monkey Mia represents a tiny speck of light:

*"This speck of light we speak of, we should never
   let it die.
We should fight to keep it glowing, every one must
   try.
We should nurture it and cherish it and always
   keep it warm.
For this little speck of light we see will one day
   be a dawn."*

DISCOVERY AND MAGIC
IN CARNARVON

CARNARVON, A PLEASANT three-hour drive north of Monkey Mia, was a tropical pocket of palms and bougainvillea flourishing amidst desert-like scrubby surroundings on three sides and bordered by the sea on the other. We'd expected to stay a day or two, but when we discovered that the caravan rates computed to $18 a day if we stayed a week, we decided to settle in. We were in the best, roomiest caravan yet. It had a large entry tent attached to it giving me a wonderful "room" in which to sit outside and write.

Sid set up the computer on the dining table in the annex and I wrote in the cool breeze--sometimes for several hours at a crack. When I needed a break, I'd stroll to the nearby cool pool. It was more like a small tank but long enough to be able to do five short strokes. As if to round out the homey comfort, the resident stray kitty cautiously approached us one day and soon graced our home curled on a cushion or draped across the computer keyboard as I worked.

Friends had looked wonderingly at us when we said we were bringing our computer camping. For the past two years wherever we found ourselves living, I had worked on my book, *Journey To Wholeness*. But as we headed north, I had misgivings and wondered how I would manage to honor the inner demands that urged me to write if we were travelling daily and camping? Instead, it was wonderful and, of course, beyond my limited imaginings.

With the advent of the caravan system, I discovered that we'd fallen into the most perfect world. Not only was I enjoying the daily travel and exploration of different areas, as well as sunning and swimming, but I also had mornings and evenings filled with purpose. When the day was too hot, cloudy or windy, Sid and I could care less. We both squirreled into our caravan sanctuary, me writing away on *Journey To Wholeness*, and Sid spending hours researching and mastering the baffling ways of our new computer.

My "office" in the caravan annex.

Our caravan park nestled between banana plantations which also grew tomatoes. Every day refuse tomatoes were deposited in yellow plastic crates next to our fence for us to take. All I could see that might prohibit them being marketed were blemishes and some suggestive shapes.

As a typical country center, Carnarvon's main street had a concrete island down its middle and bordering frontier-style covered sidewalks. There was one bakery, three or four pubs, a video store, a sparkling new post office, fax machines, centrally located men's and women's rest rooms, and a tourist bureau--in front of which groups of Aborigines were usually lolling and loudly visiting. A huge new Woolie's* complex was the hot-bed of retail activity. Thick palms, bent sideways under the furiously billowing wind, lined the main road and fascine--the levy along the bay.

During our stay only one day was calm, and even then a twinkling breeze prevented the air from being stifling. On other days the wind rollicked and whistled about our caravan, shimmying us from time to time and sounding like a raging Alaskan blizzard. We turned on the oven and baked potatoes just to counteract the forceful drafts which penetrated the caravan. The locals said that the wind was typical, but it seemed more vigorous than usual.

Bananas, tomatoes, capsicums (bell peppers), mangoes and paw paws (papaya) grew in abundance in Carnarvon. The water to support the growth of this vegetation came from the Gascoyne River, whose wide, dry red bed swathed through the town. It was an underground river with huge supplies of hidden water pumped out for irrigation. Infrequently the river coursed with water from inland rains and it usually carried water during the rainy season. People retired to Carnarvon because of the climate. It was certainly cooler there than the 40 degree (centigrade) temperatures we could expect up north. And there was a comfortable laid-back country town feeling.

As far as restaurants were concerned, the place recommended to us was the Shell Roadhouse*, five km from town where the truckers stopped to assemble their road trains*. Sid and I drove out and discovered a large brick and glass square temple-like structure on a rise surrounded by lawn and palms. It dominated a vast dirt and tarmac parking acreage which looked like a harbor of huge trucks.

The inside of the restaurant was plain but pleasant. It was divided into two sections--one with a menu and prices for truckers, another with a menu and higher prices for ordinary folks. Sid tried a mixed grill ($10) and I had a seafood platter ($14)--the grill by far the better choice. At least I got lots of fresh salad vegetables, although I had to repeatedly ask and wait for the dressing to appear. The young waitress reminded me of the waitress in the film *A Town Like Alice*-- plain and shy and sweet and none too creative.

Our challenge, we were finding, was how to be so much together and retain the freshness and desire for one another's company. Sometimes Sid and I felt crowded by each other. I know that when I get out of sorts, it's a sign that I need solitude and some quiet time with nature. But I wasn't making the effort. Sid instigated alleviating action. One night he gently massaged hand cream all over my drying body. The old feelings of his strength and of being nurtured and loved slipped back. I returned the luxury the next night, dousing him. It was non-sexual and non-demanding, a wonderful way to remember our closeness and love.

Having dinner out had also been instigated by Sid--his treat to me. It was a smart move, fun, and a good break in our routine. Again we both revived our friendship. We realized we must create those "outbreaks", otherwise we could grow stale both as individuals and as a couple.

One of our most special breaks in our routine came when Sid and I visited a banana plantation. We had expected to be taken on a mundane tour of the operation. Instead we discovered a little bit of magic--the kind of magic that happens when people let their work follow their hearts. We discovered the Munros, a young couple who have opened themselves and their plantation to the public in a bright, friendly, welcoming way.

Along with two other couples, we were led into a dense forest of rows upon rows of tall banana trees. Mr. Munro, fortyish, robust, wearing shorts, T-shirt, a leather stockman's hat, and obviously enjoying himself, told us all about bananas and graciously answered our questions which tumbled ever more readily as we learned about the fantastic art of banana growing.

The trees had huge pendulous red "flowers" hanging down. Looking up high we could see the beginning green fingers of future bananas. Each of the 15 to 20 foot high trees would yield one bunch of bananas. (A bunch consisted of about 250 bananas.) Rather than picking the bananas from that height, the grower simply cuts the tree about five feet above the ground and fells it. The tree would have died anyway, and the next generation was already evident in the form of numerous tall shoots sprouting around its base. A banana tree grows from a shoot to a full-leaved, 20-foot, fruit-bearing tree in about 15 months.

The cut-off trunks are left on the ground to decompose, forming big stringy mulch. The growers in Carnarvon fertilize with fish emulsion and urea. They have no need for insecticides because it's too hot for insects to make inroads. The bananas are picked green, washed, packed and shipped and eventually ripened in temperature controlled rooms where ethylene gas is pumped in. In the past I'd heard about the awful practice of gassing bananas. But, in fact, it is no different than what the fruit would do in the wild. The ripening banana emits ethylene gas, which encourages the ripening of the whole bunch. Mr. Munro said, "I make a good living. I get around $25 a bunch. And if you look at all these trees, that's a lot of bunches."

We passed avocados and grapefruit trees on our way to the grove of mangos, which were huge, old trees dripping with green poddy fruits that would mature into mangos around January. During harvesting Mr. Munro spends a full month perched in a cherry picker collecting them by hand. Behind the mangos, we surveyed a field of red dirt trenched with tiny banana shoots a meter apart. Mr. Munro told us that in just 15 months those young plants would look like the patch of lush and lanky trees which we had just left. Beyond the paddock of shoots were more fields abundant with grapefruit, banana, and avocado trees.

I loved the charm of the place. The Munros had developed a lovely shady, colorfully planted garden space in which to serve visitors Devonshire tea*. We sat at tables under poinciana trees with birds and flowers singing around us. Thatched straw umbrellas perched perkily over a couple of tables. Just outside the banana shed, a large table picturesque with baskets of fruit invited us to buy ruby grapefruit (40 or 50 cents each), oranges (10 cents each), and jars of prettily packed grapefruit or orange marmalade and banana butter.

Mrs. Munro smilingly brought us fresh-squeezed grapefruit juice and a plate of scones smeared generously with banana butter and topped with a thick layer of fresh whipped cream. A trim, cheerful, woman in neat jeans and plaid shirt, Mrs. Munro told us that she used to work side by side with her husband in the fields, but as the tourism developed she was delighted to spend more time orchestrating the crafts, cooking and people-meeting side of the operation.

As we savoured our treats, we perused the photo album on the table which showed banana history and other highlights of the area. These included Carnarvon's normally dry Gascoyne River in flood stage and pictures of the fluffy family cat, who was produced upon request and tolerated a cuddle. Mr. Munro flitted about the shed or the yard or the fields, frequently returning to be drawn into a friendly chat.

As we were leaving, I said to Sid, "I see a future Nut Tree here." I don't know that the Munros would wish that. The Nut Tree started as a wayside walnut stand near Sacramento, California and wound up as a multi-million dollar tourist attraction with beautifully presented produce and giftware and a fancy restaurant as well as its own airport and miniature railway. I hoped that the Munros would stop where they were and retain the laid-back friendly freshness and openness that made their place magical just as it was.

The patio at Munro's Banana Plantation.
(Photo courtesy of Good News Postcards)

THE NORTH WEST CAPE

AS SID AND I drove the swift three hours from Carnarvon to Coral Bay, our excitement rose. I read Sid the local papers and they filled our heads with enticing tales about this remote resort area. With the advent of bitumen* roads into the far north, Coral Bay on the North West Cape peninsula was gradually becoming a popular playground for vacationers because of its proximity to the West Coast Reef. The West Coast Reef was situated 30 feet offshore, and was therefore more accessible than the Great Barrier Reef*. Once we swung down the final curves of road (white chalk dirt scraped on rock) into view of the blazing beaches of Coral Bay, I was wound up with anticipation of my first experience with snorkeling.

Coral Bay consisted of an expensive but minimally appointed motel on a hill, two camping/caravan parks, one petrol station, a supply and food store, and a tin garage housing a snorkeling shop. We opted to stay at the People's Park, where a campsite cost $8 and where the manager was not grumpy as was the neighboring manager who was charging $6.

This was our first opportunity to try out our borrowed tent. Out it unfurled, and we were delighted to discover its blue roominess. Out came our new air mattresses and our borrowed cook stove, utensils and lantern. We beamed with pleasure at the way these possessions of others supplied our needs.

A few steps across the dirt road from our campground, gleamed the arc of white sand cradling the turquoise sea of Coral Bay. As soon as our tent was up, we crossed to the practically empty beach where a dozen or so people dotted the white sand or snorkeled in the water. There was a brisk breeze, but the day was very warm, and the sand was too bright to be looked at without sunglasses. I donned my swimming goggles and Sid put on his new snorkeling mask, and we plunged into the warm water.

Floating face down I viewed the world of water and fish as never before. It was beautiful and exciting. Gleaming zebra striped fish swooped just beneath me. Blossoms of yellows and oranges and pinks waved from the bottom of the sea. Schools of silver fish

37

swirled in groups of glinting clouds. I was both thrilled and eager to take advantage of this beautiful place, and I signed up with the local scuba teacher to take diving and snorkeling lessons the next day.

Alas, my snorkeling aspirations were dashed. I awoke with a horrible stiff neck so that I couldn't bend or turn, and an ear infection was coming on full blast. Before the cyclone in my ear hit full force, I managed an hour walk along the far side of the bay over to a hidden inlet where white dunes seeped down to the clear water and patrician pelicans nested along the shores. It was so secluded that I took off my bathers* and waded naked in the shimmering shallow water.

Back at the tent, my pain increased and soon I could do nothing more than lie motionless on the rubber mattress. We decided to hurry north to Exmouth where there would be doctors and a hospital. Sid broke camp and packed and at last we were ready. I sat in the car, dozy and fairly comfortable after an aspirin--which bespeaks the degree of my pain, because my policy is to give my body drugs only under the direst circumstances.

Sid was wonderfully patient with me and my grimness. Two hours later at the modern Exmouth hospital, I learned that such infections were very common because of the warm air and ocean. After leaving the doctor, we waited in the lobby for a bill to be forthcoming, but the doctor called down the corridor, "There's no bill. We're all on medicare here." This assuaged my pain somewhat, but only long enough to drive to the chemist*, where the cost of drops and pain killers was *not* on medicare--at least not for me.

Although I longed to come to rest, we tracked around to several nearly vacant caravan parks that advertised hire vans--$26 a night for a tin box with no shade and no pool or beach nearby. Thinking that surely we could do better than that, we drove a short distance out of town to King's Norcape Lodge. It had been recommended by travellers whom we'd met in Carnarvon. Although King's offered no hire vans, we hoped that maybe we'd find *some* kind of cheap accommodation. We were in luck. For $30 a night we were given a double bedroom in their staff wing. It had all the facilities similar to a caravan park--loo and showers down the hall, hot plate and utensils, twin beds sans linens--plus we were only steps from the beach and from the lodge's attractive, large freshwater pool.

Exmouth was a curiosity. As the service center for the United States Navy's radio and communications base, it was unique in the world because both U.S. and Australian Navy personnel cooperatively worked, lived, and governed the town. On our first night there, Sid and I rewarded ourselves by eating at the Mexican restaurant whose presence I'd predicted before we arrived. I *knew* there couldn't be an enclave of Americans, even in this distant Aussie outpost, without some source of Mexican food. The meals weren't cheap and had an unusual flavoring, but they were tasty and reminiscent of the food we loved.

We hunkered down to stay as cool as possible and to pass the days while my body fought the infection. I bisected my days with dosages of antibiotics, ear drops and even pain pills, and distracted myself with books. Sid, happy to have the computer freed up, busily wrote letters and studied computer manuals. We managed one long walk where we encountered more of the Northwest's characteristic wind and wide sandy beaches. We could stroll for miles and it never changed--just a different clump of seagulls or a different curve to the strand.

In town we quickly made the rounds of the one newsagency*, the two grocery shops, a bakery and a couple of drapers*. That was it although, for a small town, Exmouth was well-equipped with modern residences, offices and public buildings. These included some unique touches. The post office was, I'm sure, the only one in Australia displaying a U.S. MAIL post box in its entry. The prominence of left hand drive cars on the road revealed the presence of a foreign population. Why the Americans brought their cars with them, I couldn't guess. Maybe the navy paid for them. But they were a hazard, and had big yellow signs on the rear saying CAUTION-- LEFT HAND DRIVE.

At the town's tourist bureau we learned, from a well-done video, about the surrounding area. The Cape Range National Park was nearby, but the dirt roads would make the journey too long for a day trip. Much as we were disappointed in missing the highly touted hikes, the canoe trips and camping at the park, I was in no condition for doing much more than sitting and resting, which I could just as well do in the comfort of the air-conditioned car. So after four days, we packed up the computer, stocked the esky with refrozen water jugs, rolled up our sleeping bags and sheets, and set off for Karratha.

HAMERSLEY IRON COUNTRY

ONE HOUR AFTER leaving Exmouth, we turned on to the dirt road shortcut which the locals had assured us would pose no problem for our tires. Soft, red dust had sifted over a hard packed surface, creating only minimal ruts and crevasses. There were no other vehicles on the road as we drove along the bottom end of the North West Cape Peninsula. The land stretched horizon to horizon, dry and brushy and wavy with the pale green grasses of spinifex. The spinifex was deceitful, appearing succulent and downy, while in fact it was dry and as stiff as porcupine bristles, and completely lacking in nourishment.

Out of the spinifex rose our first sightings of the red ant hills that are typical of Australia's North. These hills were not the fluted cathedral towers frequently seen on post cards but looked more like the onion-shaped domes atop a Greek church. As we drove, the ant hills presented us with an ever-changing cavalcade of cartoon characters--red-cowled monks, dumplingish dwarfs, bulbous profiles and fat grinning faces, round, ruffly-winged owls, rotund judges presiding in red robes, and hobbits hunching across the horizon.

Behind these diverse imaginary faces, lived, of course, an entire city of ants. And a few meters further on, another, and then another. I wondered, were these cities complete within themselves? Were they aware of the existence of the others? Or did they see themselves as the beginning and end of the universe? Did they visit one another, share feasts, exchange workers or carry the news?

Occasionally we saw cattle and frail red roads leading off to what must be stations somewhere in the distance. Whenever we arrived at forks in the road, we were left to wonder and guess which would be the correct route to take for, typically, these places lacked sign posts. Our guesswork was fortunately accurate, for after a couple of hours we connected with the main road and were on our way to Karratha, the first town in the Pilbara region.

Once I had asked Katherine what was her favorite part of Western Australia. "The Pilbara," she had answered, without a pause. Now as Sid and I drove along in air conditioned comfort, the outside temperature in the forties (hundreds for us non-metric folk), I thought of Katherine, a strong-willed, independent woman who was not fazed by a bit of discomfort. We were speeding through a rugged, harsh region of sunburnt distances, which extended for almost 450,000 square kilometers from the Indian Ocean on the west to the Northern Territory on the east, from the Tropic of Capricorn in the south to the Kimberley Ranges in the north.

Although pastoralists had arrived as early as the 1860s, and gold was discovered in the 1880's, bringing about a boom period, the Pilbara remains one of the last areas in Australia to be populated and developed. In 1969, when I hitchhiked through the Pilbara, the region was going through its second "discovery and development" phase with the opening up of massive iron ore fields. Sid and I were to learn that the Pilbara was still big, wide, and raw-boned despite the influx of modern-day pioneers who came to work for the vast Hamersley mining operations and stayed on for other reasons.

The town of Karratha, 639 km from Carnarvon, didn't exist when I passed through there twenty years before. We found it, now, sprawling hot and new around a sleek air-conditioned mall-- Karratha City. From its central core fanned out the modern banks, post office, city offices and services. As we drove first to one side of town and then the other looking for caravan parks, we passed attractive modern homes, schools, a college, large medical and arts' centers, all of yellow brick and verdant with palms and lawns.

The caravan parks were either closed for the summer, full, or over-priced, so we drove 18 km further to the coastal shipping town of Dampier to "have a look"* at the youth hostel. It was ideal, situated in one of many housing blocks belonging to Hamersley Iron Contract Services. The single miners used to live there. For $12 per person a night, we each had a room with a twin bed, desk, chair and wardrobe. Down the hall were the kitchen, bathrooms and a lounge room equipped with a full size refrigerator and a good TV.

We met the only other hosteler, Fiona, a 26-year old Irish nurse, who was working and hitching her way around Australia and the world. Fiona and I immediately drifted into exchanging tales of the road. In many ways we were mirrors of each other, she travelling much as I had 20 years earlier. I was gratified to find another woman who shared the joys of hitching alone and meeting and living with

41

the Australian country people.

After travelling over 1200 km from Perth to the outback, Sid and I went straight to the Karratha mall where we spent most of Saturday strolling throughout its clean, cool, well-stocked splendor. I admit that I found it stimulating and interesting, since I loved perusing Australian products, presentations, and prices, reading the newsstand papers (The Berlin Wall had come down!) and sampling new tastes in the bakeries and shops.

I also liked Dampier, rough and red, and presided over by huge shipyards and iron ore processing plants. These I remembered from 1969, having driven right into the heart of the plant with the two electricians who had given Matthew and me a lift. Different now were the several blocks of well-made brick houses sprouting green lawns and palms amidst a beautiful natural landscape of heaped jumbles of rusty rock.

The town buildings covered a small hill which followed the course of the bay. Attractive palm-strewn sandy beaches lined the shore, many peppered with acres of dark black pudding-shaped rocks. The turquoise water was dotted throughout with rust red islands--part of the Dampier archipelago--some sprawling long and flat, some squatting round and lumpy. The most eye-catching island, however, loomed directly across the bay, dominated by a long pyramid of red ore and a pair of huge science fiction-looking cranes belonging to the Hamersley Iron operations.

On the morning we arrived to take the Hamersley Iron tour, we discovered that it was the tour leader's day off. The one employee in the attractive cool office building was the public relations lady, catching up on newsletters. She kindly opened the large, cushy film room and turned on the tour film for a private showing. We were mightily impressed with the quality of the presentation as well as with the story of Hamersley Iron, which began in the early 1960's.

Satisfied with our armchair tour, we readied ourselves to leave. But the lady said that she could spare some time and that she herself would be happy to take us up to the lookout. We drove in her air conditioned station wagon across the causeway into the loading grounds, cruising under mammoth mountains of red ore waiting to be shipped. Each represented different levels of mixing--fine and coarse--according to the grades specified by customers. Paralleling the road a huge conveyer--rusty red as was everything else on this site--reached tentacle-like fingers into the long pyramidal piles. The ore travelled on this conveyor to the holds of ships. Special sieves on the conveyor allowed the fine ore to escape so it could be carried back to the pile where once again it did the job of mixing ore. Eventually there would pile up an overstock of fine ore and that would simply be dumped.

As our hospitable driver escorted us to the lookout area, she pointed out piles of splintered saplings and explained that these had been uprooted in the last cyclone. When we climbed the stairs to the lookout, she pointed to a large, silver, onion-like ball lying on the ground, and explained that it was the local radar cyclone detector. It had been blown off in the last cyclone and had not yet been replaced.

Below us, on a rust colored area as vast as several football fields, red dust spewed forth from behind mighty yellow trucks moving red ore from one pile to another. Amazingly, only five or six men controlled the entire operation. We wondered what happened to all those ore piles when a cyclone hit and learned that instead of being blown away, the rain settled the ore down more solidly. Pointing to long funnels running down the sides of the ore piles, our guide told us they had been formed by the torrential rains five months before.

On the way out, we stopped at the railway platform and watched as gigantic machines, lifting and tipping two boxcars at a time, emptied the ore. The ore shot into several large bins and was piped upward to a huge belt carrying it to the various piles awaiting shipping.

After a very informative hour, our benefactress deposited us back at the Tourist Gathering Center. In response to Sid's request for some kind of brochure, she disappeared into a room and returned with two tiny cellophane packets of iron ore and an armful of books. They were editions of the Hamersley Diary which the company had once printed annually, but had ceased to do. Thanking her, we asked if everyone received such beautiful momentos and learned that, no, this was exceptional.

That afternoon driving to Port Hedland with our hitchhiker passenger, Fiona, I read this treasury of books, blessing our unnamed angel for supplying us with them. Each book treated different aspects of the Pilbara region--*Water, Reflections of the People, Mining,* and *Sea Life.* They were extraordinarily well produced, presenting a most colorful and intriguing insight into the area.

The book about people particularly interested me as it offered stories about the pastoralists and gold miners who pioneered in the late 1800's and the iron ore miners who pioneered beginning in the 1960's. The Pilbara saga was one of hardship, camaraderie, and the perseverance of people who had to cope with cyclones, minimal water, as well as communication and transportation problems in a harsh region where the average summer temperatures are around 40 degrees Celsius.

It was difficult to believe the hardships and the primitive conditions that had existed as late as the 1960's, and to realize how, even then, as I had been vagabonding about Dampier and the Tom Price mine, I had fallen into an exceptional place and time. Just as I had loved it, these early Hamersley employees did too. Stories abounded about the endurance, fellowship, pranks and the pioneer spirit that existed in the sixties. And the underlying message from the stories and from those who were interviewed whispered, "It's not like it was."

ROADHOUSES, PORT HEDLAND AND THE FISHERMEN'S REST

DURING THE ENTIRE 235 km drive to Port Hedland, there was only one roadhouse, Whim Creek, to offer travelers a break from the long journey. It sat in the middle of nowhere, sun-baked and offering minimal shade from sparse, straggly trees. Roadhouses were merely hot oases, but on this northern trip they offered welcome, much anticipated breaks in the long hours of driving across the dry, scrubby distances. It was the roadhouses that made travel possible in such parts of Australia, linking distant towns with a life line of petrol and water. Petrol became almost a luxury the further north we drove, starting out costing 58 cents a liter and topping out at 85 cents a liter. That translated to about three dollars and fifty cents per gallon in American money.

Once the car was filled with petrol, we'd park it in the wispy shade of a fragile tree or under a corrugated tin shade port if we were lucky enough to find such a spot. Then we'd straggle through a path of flies and heat into the roadhouse to entertain ourselves by looking at the latest version of the same post cards, books and magazines, videos, cassettes, auto supplies, groceries, and souvenir cartoons, mugs, and T-shirts that we'd seen at the last stop.

In general, roadhouses were all-encompassing complexes providing, in varying degrees, motel rooms, caravan park accommodations, take-out and restaurant food, pub, toilets, showers and supplies. Some, such as the spacious new green and yellow British Petroleum stations, were very plastic but clean, and air-conditioned. They were nothing like the steaming corrugated and fibro* family-run affairs of 20 years ago. A few roadhouses, though, were still family-leased and had kept their original slap-dash, dishevelled tin and fibro look. Interiors were cooled by desultory overhead fans, and rough dark wood counters were piled high with plastic wrapped slices of homemade cakes and pies.

It was not unusual to find a worn man or woman drooping amidst the take-out paraphanelia--coolers full of beverages, shelves and counters exhibiting candy bars, (further north, candy bars were more often stored in the cooler) and stainless steel warming trays under hot lights displaying fried foods such as sausage rolls*, dim sims*, rissoles*, chips, chicken or fish.

Racks of pies and pasties could be seen through the window of a nearby oven, and on the wall behind the counter would be a board listing the made-to-order food such as sandwiches, fish and chips and hamburgers. Our favorite, which we chose every time, was a hamburger "with the lot." The price, which usually varied from two to four dollars, was no indication of the quality of the food. There was always something different about the presentation. The basics included a huge patty, bun, fried egg, variations of tomato, shredded lettuce, beetroot or carrot, condiments, and perhaps a pickle. Most of these were so big that Sid and I would split one and feel well filled. Usually they were delicious.

Three hours after leaving Karratha, we arrived in Port Hedland which was more dismal than I remembered it. Along the waterfront, red piles of ore awaited loading on to ships, and dust from these piles was spewed by the boiling wind into every crack and cranny of the town and painted every surface red. Thick red layers of dust coated our car, clothes and skin.

After dropping Fiona with the friendly manager at the run-down tin can of a Backpackers Hostel,* we drove a short distance down a dusty street of mostly closed shops to the Fishermen's Rest restaurant. Paul and Heather, the owners of the establishment, were friends of the Perey's and they were expecting us. They graciously invited us to stay in their spare room and immediately sat us down at a booth, offering us tea, coffee, Coke or whatever we wanted, and we talked for the rest of the afternoon.

In the evening Paul and Heather led us to a table covered with a lace cloth in the empty formal dining room and treated us to one of their delicious fish and chips meals. They managed to join us for a few moments in between taking care of their customers. The deli had such close quarters that Sid and I would only be in the way if we tried to help out, so after dinner we crossed the back patio to our hosts' outdoor lounge room. Opening the red dust-coated door, we entered a pretty screen-enclosed room scattered with chairs and couches. Making ourselves comfortable on the bright, floral printed cushions, we settled in to watch TV while Paul and Heather continued working.

It was a "good" night--Paul and Heather were busy until ten o'clock. When they joined us, they collapsed onto the couches and we talked long into the night--about bliss and work and fears, about finances, their hopes and the stresses of their life. They wanted freedom but, tied down to their business, they couldn't see how to achieve it. Sid and I listened and asked some leading questions hoping that their own answers would bring solutions, or, at least, fresh ways of viewing things. I don't think they heard the questions.

Finally, we said good night and went to our guest room. It was a closet sized space just big enough for two foam mats side by side on the floor. Fortunately we had been given a fan to catch the sparse breeze that managed to trickle in through the screen door and single window. Outside we could hear the roaring of the wind and the generators running the restaurant's freezer room.

Our hearts went out to these kind, hard working people who so willingly shared with us their hopes, dreams and frustrations. We appreciated their hospitality and their repeated offers to stay longer and come again. But we were eager to get to Broome, so we rolled up our reddening bedding and, with a gift of ice slabs from Paul's freezer, we set off for that fabled outpost.

BACK TO BROOME

GOING BACK TO a beloved place, or person, can be wonderful or awful. So it was with trepidation that I anticipated renewing my love affair with Western Australia's tropical outpost of Broome. Certainly in 21 years *I* had changed. How would I handle Broome's "progress"?

As we entered Broome, the tropical foliaged streets glowed orange in the November sundown, and I excitedly pointed out the boab trees to Sid. I'd always remembered and loved those bottle shaped trees that seemed to characterize the fantastical landscapes of fairy tales.

We settled in at the Broome Vacation Village, a modern caravan park on the outskirts of town. Due to the pilot strike and the slow summer season, prices were slashed in half, and for $25 a night we were given a roomy, cream and white brick chalet equipped with a queen-size bed and a kitchen with electric pans, kettles and utensils.

The first thing we did was to make a beeline to the lighted pool. It was a real resort affair with palms arcing up from a central boulder bedecked island and warm water from an upper pool flowing over tiles into the large, gracefully curving lower lagoon.

"How did we get so lucky?" we asked each other.

"What a way to go. This is the life."

Smiling at our good fortune, we softly swam across the glowing lime-green pool, while above us palms shimmered under a cantaloup yellow moon rising in the velvet sky.

I happened into Broome in 1969 after I broke my big toe playing the Golliwog* in a play at the Perth Children's Theater. Temporarily unable to ply my rounds as a wine house waitress, I was not sufficiently crippled to turn down an invitation to join two men travelling to Broome. Tim, a geologist, was sent to explore the Broome coast on a pearling lugger* which his mining company had refurbished. Matthew, my film-making friend, and I tagged along. It took us three days of jolting in a jeep over mostly dirt roads to reach Broome. There we visited the crews aboard various luggers and met the captain of the then-sagging pearling fleet. After Tim had sailed away, Matthew and I hitchhiked back to Perth, arriving there lobster-red from the road's unrelenting dust.

Broome had been on the map for years. As the center of Australia's pearling industry, divers converged on Broome from Indonesia, the Philippines, China, Malaysia and Japan to dive alongside Australians and Aborigines on the continent's northwest coast. At one time there were 350 pearling luggers in Broome's Roebuck Bay. Pearls were few, but the iridescent shell of the pearl oysters sold well on the world markets-- for such items as combs, buttons and jewelry--until plastics displaced them. When I came through Broome in the 1960's, luggers lay rotting in the mangrove swamps, and only a few pearlers remained to man the dozen or so surviving boats. Nowadays, several companies are sending out luggers to collect live shell for the pearl farms up and down the coast. These farms grow cultured pearls that are even bigger than those produced in Japanese waters.

The diverse accumulation of cultures in this remote outback region of Australia made Broome a town with a surprisingly beguiling character. I fell in love with the bulbous boab and other tropical trees, the British colonial corrugated architecture, the beautiful multi-racial children, and the friendliness of the outback locals. Now Sid and I discovered, over twenty years later, that Broome has become The Place To Go.

The first day in Broome we walked past the dilapidated jetty where Matthew and I once sat for several hours alongside the Aborigine girls watching and waiting for the tide to rise so the luggers could depart. The mangroves had taken over the little harbor, and I could no longer see the opening where the luggers turned out to sail on the turquoise sea. Just behind the jetty stood the same dock building in front of which the Aborigines had gathered, smiling shyly and joking with us. And there was the porch where the ebony man carved a boab nut with a rusty knife and then gave it to me.

Steps away, the street displayed an entire new face. Pretty palm-lined rows of shops, white corrugation with red trim, brashly gleamed a few strides down from the grease and rust of cargo sheds and ship works. Mushroom quiches, pearls, mother of pearl jewelry, fish leather accessories and fancy fashions and prices clamored from inside cool display rooms. The jet set tourist trade had come to Broome.

But it was not depressingly dismal. The rest of the town center was only a trifle trendy. Around the corner, past the disappointing offerings of the Kimberly Bakery, lay the main street, a mix of mostly old, dishevelled buildings and a crease of spanking new ones. The Chinese general store still creaked top-heavy with an improbable mix of merchandise. There was a chock-a-block news agency, whose stock of magazines and papers would credit any Sydney establishment. The "Oldest Picture Garden In The World" hid behind a padlock and peeling paint. A picture garden, we learned, is a semi-roofed area for movies where people used to sink into cavernous folding chairs, evidently designed to accommodate the courting habits of teenage couples. The street was empty except for chatting merchants and a few straggling shoppers.

The cosmopolitan mix of races who had come to Broome following the lure of pearling fortunes appealed to me. Just as they had twenty years ago, Japanese, Filipino, Chinese, Aborigines, Malays continued to contribute bits and pieces of their cultures to the melting pot of this outback outpost. Sarongs and sate, incense and boab nuts, mingled with beer and stockmen's hats on shop shelves. I loved the exotic flavor, the strangely styled tin houses with corrugated roofs overshadowed by big-flowered trees and shaggy palms, the profusion of brilliant tropical colors, the big-bottomed boabs beside fine-leaved gums, and the buildings-- including the corner phone boxes--with oriental, uptipped iron roofs.

A short drive away at Cable Beach, Sid and I visited the crocodile farm where we saw crocodiles lounging in swampy pens. At feeding time they would lumber into view and gulp down whole (dead) chickens to the enthusiastic accompaniment of clicking tourist cameras.

When we had had enough of crocodile watching, we strolled on to the spectacular Pearl Coast Zoological Gardens. Here, as at the Monterey Bay Aquarium in California, people can join the animals in their habitats. Hundreds of colorful birds luxuriated in roomy, thatch-covered cages, many of which were lush with bamboo, trees and running water. We entered a huge wire-domed, walk-in aviary with rock banks, waterfalls, ponds and profuse vegetation. As we ambled along a high wooden trestle that sloped up and down and curved around the interior of the aviary, we human visitors could meet the birds at their level. The zoo's numerous trestle pathways also allowed us to venture into other enclosures where we could observe at close hand such exotic animals as African deer, nyalla, and other rare, range species.

I took many pictures, wanting to share with others the way this marvelous place honored its animal and bird residents. The zoo was inspired by Lord McAlpine, whose name crops up often in Broome literature. I was curious to know more about this man. Seeing the love of animals and preservation of endangered species which the zoo represented, I thought that I would like him.

From the zoo we moved on to the climax of our day--riding the camels of Cable Beach. On our way to the camels, we passed the attractive oriental style Cable Beach Resort--looking very much like a page from a Bali brochure. This, too, was a brainchild of Lord McAlpine's. Again, I liked what I saw. It was tasteful, elegant, attractive, and in keeping with the local ambience--a gem rather than a sore on the landscape. Certainly it changed the face and the texture of Broome, attracting a class of folks who would never otherwise appear in that dusty outpost. I couldn't judge it, though. I could only admire the beauty and taste of the place and, as I did with Broome, accept the inevitability of change.

THE CAMELS OF CABLE BEACH

ALONG WITH RIDING an elephant and cuddling a baby panda bear, riding a camel has been on my list of things to do before I die. At Broome's Cable Beach, I had my chance to check off the camel ride.

It was four o'clock in the afternoon when Sid and I stepped onto the beach and approached the train of six camels kneeling in the sand like lego toys, one behind the other. A single strand of cotton rope casually looped the lead camel to a thin iron fence post thrust into the ground. Three children in yellow and navy school uniforms rollicked amongst the great beasts, petting and hugging them and handing out offerings of torn-up scrub grass. The camels seemed unperturbed.

Sid and I circuitously advanced, carefully extending hands for sniffing and then chanced a pat on the neck. I remembered those softly elegant camel hair coats we used to see in stores and realized that the name refers solely to the color, for petting a camel is akin to caressing a brillo pad.

The three lead camels each had a peg protruding from a nostril. A string from the peg ran down to the halter rope, which was looped to the camel immediately ahead. I wondered, couldn't man have contrived gentler methods of insuring the cooperation of these great animals?

A narrow, golden hippie boy descended the rock steps to the beach. His only attire was a pair of tie-dyed black levies, splashed with a fluff of scarlet mysteriously appearing from somewhere in his pants front, and a turquoise scarf twisted round his stringy, sunstreaked hair. Sid and I joined the handful of tourists and watched with interest as this young T.E. Lawrence tended the camels. With deliberate movements he dropped thin cloths across the leather and metal structures which made up the saddles. Twice, a camel rose bringing the others quickly along to their feet. "Lawrence" calmly gestured them down, and each obediently knelt, legs collapsing like popsicle sticks underneath their large bodies.

Boarding time was a noisy affair. Passengers squealed, chattered and nervously joked. I asked "Lawrence" if it made any difference on which end of the camel the heavier person sat. He said it was better if I rode in the front. So I sat astride the bars of the saddle while Sid haunched round the hairy hump. Suddenly Sid shot skyward, while I dipped precariously groundward. Then, with a massive lunge, the camel heaved up on his front legs and we were airborne.

"Lawrence" loosely looped the lead rope of the front camel around his wrist and, with his ever-present soft smile, started walking us toward the center of the wide, white beach. There was chatter and laughter from the ladies behind us as we accustomed ourselves to this one-of-a-kind form of movement. Our shadows strung like accordion cutouts undulating across the sand, Sid bobbing up, I bobbing down, and on down the line. I liked the looseness of the rhythm and allowed myself to sway sideways and

The camels of Cable Beach.

53

forwards with the camel, thinking how beneficial for the spine such loose undulations must be.

Sway. Swoop. Sway. Swoop. Up. Down. Me up. Sid down. After the smiles and the laughter and a half hour of undulating along the beach, we noticed the chafing of our thighs. I thought about the Three Wise Men and was thankful I wasn't one of them. I felt the hardness of the saddle through the thin cloth and remembered Robyn Davidson's book *Tracks*, and appreciated even more her endurance on her camel trek across Australia's center.

"Lawrence" kept a steady, slow pace, never looking back. I draped my left leg across the pommel--ah, relief. Then the other leg. Sid too, squirmed and shifted positions on his perch. After an hour, I thought we'd surely received our money's worth. Did we really need to travel the WHOLE length of the beach? Surely we all would have been quite content to climb aboard, have our picture taken, take a turn or two around the beach, and then head off for drinks at the Cable Beach Hotel. The romance of seeing the sunset by camelback was waning, and the damn sun was still halfway out of the water.

Memories of five years before rushed over me, contrasting the aliveness of this day with the seeming dead days of the past. Here I was, riding a camel alongside the Indian Ocean, salt-laden air skimming my bare, brown legs and healthy body. It was a moment of celebration, recognizing the rebirth it represented. I was vividly alive in a drama of joy, vibrancy, and exotica that five years before had seemed impossible--the stuff of life for others, but not for me, diagnosed with multiple sclerosis and struggling to gain health and some kind of spiritual harmony.

In fascination, I continually looked down the camel's legs to where its feet padded skillet-sized imprints in the sand. It was unlike any foot I'd ever seen. The buff-colored hair of the legs darkened and reddened around the ankles. Fluidly the foot planted itself securely in the sand. It was large as a fry pan, cloven in two, with two very dainty forward nails. The bottom of the foot was as smooth as the sole of a moccasin. How had such an amazing design, structure and function all come together? Only from some source beyond imagination, I concluded.

At last "Lawrence" led our little band in a large, wide turn, and soon we were heading northward, the sun sinking slowly over our left shoulders. And then there was a burst of shimmering sky and water and the sun sank like a stone in the horizon before we could comprehend its passage. It was six o'clock.

Swaying, plodding, rhythmically rising and falling atop the docile camels, we approached rest. We, not the animals, displayed barn sickness. Their stride never varied. At the base of the stairs, like a collapsing house of cards, they each knelt, one behind the other. At last we got off and stood on solid sand slightly bowlegged.

"Lawrence" quickly gathered the blankets into a pile, lashed them atop one camel, climbed aboard the lead camel and set off for their night's resting place a mile or so away in the bush. Leaving these beautiful animals and the wide beach, our little group turned toward the Cable Beach Resort and found its way to those waiting drinks.

THE BUNGLE BUNGLES

AFTER A WEEK in Broome, we reluctantly said good-by to our little chalet, the beaches and the camels. The car was packed, ready for our 750 km drive to Halls Creek. But first, we made a call to Katherine to find out about the house sitting prospect in Albany. Before I could ask about it, Katherine said, "It's for December 16th to January 13th. Can you do it?" We excitedly said, Yes! and with that new plan, the course of our future changed.

As we headed out of Broome into the dry landscape dotted now and again with magnificent boab trees, the adventure sap rose within us. Excitedly discussing our rapidly changing plans, we agreed that we could not consider travelling further north than Halls Creek. It was already November 22, and Perth, not to mention Albany, Western Australia's most southerly town, were a long way off. Driving from Broome to Halls Creek only to turn around and come right back seemed slightly silly. However, we were determined to reach the most distant objective of our trip--the Bungle Bungles. We'd first heard about the Bungles from the Pereys who described the airplane flight over these rock formations as an incredible experience not to be missed. So we went ahead with our plan to see this unique place.

After an eight-hour drive, we arrived at Halls Creek in the mid-afternoon. One advantage of travelling in the hot season was that there were virtually no tourists to contend with. The local flight service, Crocodile Air, had two seats available on the next morning's flight over the Bungles. There was also plenty of room at the pub, where we settled comfortably into one of the backpacker rooms. For $15 per person, we each had a bunk bed with pink sheets, access to the pub's large pool, and the greatest luxury since leaving Perth--our own bathroom in the room.

The next morning, looking down upon the earth's endless expanse from my seat in the small Cessna, I thought of the term "The Timeless Land" which is so often applied to Australia. The land extended, baked and dried, apparently unchanging--Timelessness itself. I knew, of course, that rains sometimes engorged the dry beds that wound like shrivelled veins across the puckered earth. Willy willies* whirled by like dervishes in the dust. Ants created colonies. But the essence of the land continued awesomely and endlessly, repeating cycles of unmonitored change over ageless eons.

Waiting, seemingly forbidding, yet strikingly full of character, were the Bungle Bungles, rising like dark clouds out of a pale pink sea. Their scale was beyond perception. We skimmed above red mounds creased by knife edged gorges, bleeding red wounds in a convoluted maze. Further on the gorges gave way to beehives-- striated layers upon layers of domes, like thousands of huge inverted marble-swirled cupcakes--all the striations exactly level from one end of the formation to the other.

Another area yawned with stairstep-like gullies bristling with tall, long-necked palms. Shades of pale greens dotted the high ledges and the curving hollows. Barely discernable pools of recent rain water glistened darkly from gully shadows. Our pilot told us that no wild life existed down there. The Bungles were as inaccessible to animals as they were to man.

We had heard that the Bungles had only been discovered in the 1980's. Our pilot told us that the locals had known about the Bungles, flew over them, and thought them to be "interesting." But no one made anything of them until the eighties when tourists started to fly over.

The unusual name, we learned, originated from a station outpost nearby and the formations adopted the name. Where the original name of the outpost came from no one knew. Even the Aborigines had never been there, said our pilot. Only now were they, too, joining the Bungle bandwagon. The government had declared the area a park and gave pieces of it to the Aborigines to control. An airstrip was being constructed, and by the next season, tourists would be able to fly in, spend 24 hours with a guide and fly out.

Turning back toward Halls Creek, we flew toward the interminable pink haze and the withered web of the baking land. When we'd driven across it, it looked so uniform. Now from the air, we saw distinctions, landmarks within the station kingdoms--a horseshoe bend here, a crinkled hillside there. After the intense color of the Bungles, the expanse looked faded, bleached as if too

The Bungle Bungles.

long in the sun. Intermingling with the uniform patterns of pale, sparse trees were the conical shapes and shadows of ant hills, and the puckering of veins of creek beds whose only claim to being a creek was to carry water for a few hours after a rare rain. Nothing moved, but thin tracks wove a fine-fanned pattern to and from occasional water troughs. The land sat waiting, as if nothing changed--as if it was Timelessness itself.

*   *   *

The next day, beginning our race with time, we left Halls Creek, turning our car south toward Broome and to Albany, 3440 km away.

WE ZOOM THROUGH WITTENOOM

TWO DAYS AFTER leaving Halls Creek, we left Broome for the last time. It was unlikely that I would return--just as it was unlikely that I would pass through any of those West Australian hamlets again. But saying goodbye to Broome was different. Something about the place touched me and tugged forth a response. Reluctantly I drove away, knowing that no more boabs were likely to crop up between Broome and Perth, and the end of my life. It was the boabs that I had remembered over the years and, incredibly, I *had* returned. Now I left Broome again, slightly sad. *It must be the boabs*, I thought to myself. *I'll miss those fairytale trees.*

Besides our need to hasten south, neither one of us wanted to see Port Hedland's dismal dusty face again. We quickly hurried on to the turnoff that would take us to Wittenoom 300 km to the south. Most people visit Wittenoom in the winter (April through October) but we were so close, and had heard so much about the rugged Gorges sequestered in the nearby Hamersley Ranges, that we decided to take our chances with the heat.

We had anticipated a quick, three-hour drive. The first two hours went swiftly, but then the detours started. Shunted right and left along miles of dirt, for two hours we crisscrossed the paved road under construction, road crews occasionally clattering alongside in huge machinery. Directional signs were as obscure as they were absent and often we weren't certain which track to follow.

Gradually the land grew more hilly. We dipped often into dry creek beds shimmering with white barked gums. The Hamersley Ranges loomed ahead, first violet, then straw colored, then red boned with the five o'clock sun carving intense blue shadows across their faces. After a final 32 km of dirt road alongside the northern slopes of the Hamersleys, we were in Wittenoom--population under 60.

"David Doud's Bungarra Bivouac," the Backpacker's lodge which we'd frequently seen advertised, bulged with hostelers and backpackers. There was no room for us so we left the young and sweaty crowd in the cluttered, ramshackle old house and looked elsewhere. We inspected the caravan park, the abandoned corrugated convent (a convent in Wittenoom!), the dreary Holiday Homes cottages which offered fans but had no windows that opened, the pub where they charged $70 for a room, and circled back to pitch our tent in the caravan park by the light of our lantern. Even with darkness, the heat was oppressive. Throughout the night dry, hot blasts of wind fluttered our tent like a constant cat pouncing on a paper bag.

The next morning, awaking as usual around five o'clock, I sat down to write in the first light of the sun. Before me squatted the uninspiring view of the dingy clapboard ablutions building, settled slightly askew amidst red dirt and a valiantly striving "lawn". Two red-rust clothes lines, also askew, drooped between us. Stringy gums were scattered sparsely throughout the rest of the caravan park, and the one hire van was already frying in the hot sun. For once I was grateful for the wind and for the clouds which were stringing gauzy filters across the sky, creating a degree's difference in the temperature. To my left, the Hamersleys rose like a train of round box cars--massive, heavy, red boned rock poking through a threadbare veiling of faded green spinifex.

During the night in the stifling tent, unable to reach any semblance of coolness, I periodically wondered why we were there, withering in a stuffy tent under dry furnace blasts in a barren desert country. Cool and pretty places waited for us two days' drive away. Yet here I was and with me, like Sancho Panza, was my loyal Sid. The discomfort, though, was slight compared to that endured by others about whom I'd read.

And, too, even in the furnace blast of the morning heat, I was thankful for the freedom that allowed me to experience such "exotic" places. But I also thought, *We'll see how I feel after three days*. David Doud's first opening for his acclaimed tour of the gorges was not until Sunday. So we would be two days "cooling our heels" in century heat*.

Driving that morning along the Wittenoom Gorge on the only sealed road in the area, Sid and I congealed like two eggs baking in the oven of the car. It was 40 C (106 F) in the shade, 45 C in the parked car. The road took us past three different pools of water, each at the base of a red wall of rock. Feeling like Moses in the bullrushes, we soaked in the green water of Cathedral Pool. A few goosebumps gathered on my skin and for once I welcomed them. Within minutes of emerging from the pool we were blown dry by the furnace winds. Clambering about the hot mud-encrusted rocks, swatting flies and sweating, we were in need of the pool again before we reached the car.

The road fizzled out into a dry, red dead end. Along the way, we passed the long blue skirt of the asbestos tailings draping from the gorge floor hundreds of feet straight up. Beyond, on a farther hillside with asbestos spilling straight down, we could see the tin shed, tiny from that distance, that must have been the headquarters for the mine in its heyday. I couldn't imagine climbing and working and mining in this heat in pre air-conditioned days. Yuk!

Parked in a shady spot, sweating and wildly waving at flies, we asked ourselves again, what were we doing here? Why would anyone choose to live in a place where blankets are relics and one was never sure whether one had turned on the right faucet, because hot water flowed from both taps? A place where the wind was so strong that we dared not set up our gas stove outside, but installed it instead on the counter in the laundry room? A place where people surrendered the clean-up battle to red dust so pervasive that it crusted the shower floors and soap dishes between use, and fingers came away red-coated from counters and ledges and panes?

Wittenoom is a paradox. It is at once dying and growing. After the asbestos mines shut down, the population of several thousand dwindled. Today weeds choke rubbly fields littered with decayed structures just as in dead mining towns of California's Sierras. At the same time, the tourist industry is booming with busses bundling in more than 70,000 tourists during the winter season. I doubt that many tourists stay the night. The accommodations consisted of just what we had encountered on our first night. The one old pub seemed to cater to its established clientele, and was not very friendly to strangers.

Still sweating, but out of the sun at least, Sid and I took shelter in the souvenir shop, and killed an hour nearly dozing in the pleasant drone of the shop lady's monologue. As the town's self-appointed tourist bureau, she delighted in pointing at and outlining maps with a red pointed pen. She eagerly filled us in on everything: the state of the roads, the stupidity of the Shire, the health department reports showing that in 1979 Perth had more asbestos in the air than Wittenoom. She talked about a current state-wide news item--the teachers in Perth who wanted to close down a school. It had had an asbestos roof for twenty years, and they considered it a health hazard. Our shopkeeper concluded that there were always crazies like that around.

Having exhausted our visit to the souvenir shop, we wondered what was left to do for another day and a half while waiting for Dave's Gorge Tour. We could have driven ourselves to the gorges and bush-walked to the pools, but neither we, nor our car tires, were made of stern enough stuff to venture forth in such boiling heat on gravel roads and isolated tracks. Returning to our tent site, we nudged the car as closely to a dense shade tree as possible, flung all four doors and windows open to the hot breeze, and reclined the seats as far as they'd go. Armed with books and water, we prepared to spend the next two days sitting there in pools of sweat and flies.

Sid looked as close to a corpse as I'd ever seen him, his malaise intensified, no doubt, by skipping his morning coffee. When Sid says it's too hot to drink coffee, it's HOT--so hot, in fact, that when we set our thermometer on the ground for ten minutes, the mercury went right off the register. Only the crows, seemingly unruffled by wind and heat, moved in the landscape, strutting and pecking at the red ground beside us. Flies swam in on the breeze, dunked in our sweat, and staggered out. We talked about our situation...Three nights and two days more of this. Were we mad? We'd seen the numerous gorge photos in the hostel and shop walls. Wasn't that enough?

Yes, it was, we agreed. Within moments, we decided that we were either not as hardy or not as masochistic as the locals, gathered our tent, and evacuated Wittenoom.

TO THE SOUTH

WITH THE RETREAT from Wittenoom, our spirits rose. It was sheer ecstasy to sit in the air conditioned car, sailing along the gracefully curving, wide paved road to Newman. The small town of Newman sprouted modern and green beside the dusty pit of the mighty Mt. Newman mine. There would not be a tour of the mine for a few days, so after a blissful night in an air conditioned caravan and many refreshing dunks in the cold caravan park pool, we struck out the next morning on Highway 95 South.

Had there been a comfortable and interesting place to stop for a spell, we'd have done so, but amidst the barrenness and heat, keeping moving appealed to us the most. Sid, who preferred driving to being a passenger, grew ragged. The driving was difficult because the main highway was demanding and dangerous. Although the bumpy pavement had a line down the middle, it was really only one wide lane, often merging roughly with the gravel shoulder. Slight inclines and curves made it impossible to anticipate whether or not a vehicle was approaching from the opposite direction. Road trains* barrelled along, giving no quarter. A driver who didn't slow down in time, could wind up careening out of control on the gravel shoulder. I, however, had an easy ride, sitting cool and cross legged reading Alec Guiness's autobiography, *Blessings in Disguise*, hoping that some of his droll style and sparkle would rub off on me.

Outside, the baking bush was ever endless. Roadhouses were at least an hour, sometimes two, apart. One place Sid and I particularly noticed, since it depicted such a typical scene of roadhouse life. We pulled up beside a wide, low-roofed station style building. Three men sat on the verandah drinking beer and chatting while the thin woman manager flew dejectedly back and forth from the petrol pump to the back yard trying to get the generator to work so the gas would pump. Nearby a microwave tower beamed telephone service to this station and beyond, making the straggly miles of telephone poles obsolete.

Riding along, encapsulated in our comfortable car, I thought about what I was learning from this travel experience. I had learned

The North-South road.

that Sid and I were a good team. We both liked the same things in our travel--seeking comfort, simplicity and bargains, yet not refraining from spending a bit more on special dinners, better accommodations or air flights. I learned that my travel took on more meaning when I wrote about it; that I felt fulfilled spending long hours at the keyboard striving to describe places and experiences for friends. I learned that I didn't want to travel without some sort of compelling project or purpose. Without the letters and writings, there'd be a gap, a void, in my reason for travelling about.

After a six hour drive from Newman we arrived in Mt. Magnet at sundown. Since the one caravan park offered no hire vans, we stopped at the Mt. Magnet Hotel--an old building typical of thousands of Australian pubs, with wide verandahs encircling the two stories, and a downstairs bar and dining room--cavernously plain and somewhat dingy. Searching for the reception desk, Sid and I threaded our way through the throng of noisy bar patrons, feeling slightly uncomfortable--like foreign fish in a very small, intimate pond. The bar was packed with the town's miners, men who had come to Mt. Magnet to take advantage of the last months of mining before the government's new gold tax went into effect.

After a lot of shuffling of papers and two trips up and down the long stairway to look at rooms, the hotel manager at last seemed to figure out what to do with us. We accepted the only room with a window that opened, realizing that we would be trading peace for air. It was Saturday evening and already music, raucous chatter and laughter assailed us from the bar. For $30 we had twin beds in a tall-ceilinged room at the top of the stairs. Toilets and bathrooms were a minute's walk down the hallway of face-to-face doors. Listlessly we munched a few carrots and rye crackers from our esky and then fell exhausted into our beds.

Pushing along the next day on the last leg of our trip, we eagerly anticipated arriving in Perth. Impatiently, we watched the 560 km slowly ticking by. More and more little hamlets dotted our route. The temperature cooled to 26 degrees (75 F) and the terrain changed to gentle hills and rolling grain fields. With the change of landscape the large trees appeared. Troops of thick-trunked gums marched along the floodways or the river valleys. Tall, slender gums reached like ballerinas across corps of corpulent shrubs. Other varieties lined the road unfurling themselves like green parachutes tethered on filigreed branches.

The swelling strains of Ray Lynch's *Deep Breakfast* always seem right for any place I happen to be in nature. The music accompanied us across the northwest scrub, sharpening our awareness of its barren grandeur. Now, nearing Perth, the music carried us along as we skimmed over the wild yet softened landscape. Trees and farms and fields rolled away from the tree-shaded road. My spirit inflated when I once again saw the big trees. Only now, as I returned to their presence, did I realize how much I'd missed them.

In Perth we took lodging at a youth hostel since the Pereys were busy, but we visited with them during our brief two-day stay. They told us that instead of one house sitting prospect in Albany there were now two houses to be taken care of, and the first one would be available within the week. Once again we bundled ourselves and our gear into our car and set off to the south.

The rural countryside was appealing. Noble gums marched like stalwart oaks across wide, well-groomed paddocks. Trim horses, sleek stables and picturesque stud farms abounded. Ponds, lakes and estuaries sparkled. Towns, services or hamlets were no more than 40 km apart--usually much less. We appreciated the contrast of this friendly, soft, receptive landscape which was so different from the hot, demanding north which we had recently experienced.

The southwest, despite its beauty, was actually a little too cool for our taste. We missed our routine of wearing shorts by day and needing only single sheets at night. Fortunately, the youth hostels we stopped in weren't full and, at each one, I managed to borrow piles of spare bedding from empty bunks.

One place we stopped was at Tingledale youth hostel, a working sheep farm 15 km from the Coastal Highway. Its beautiful, pristine farmland sprawled high up on rolling hills surrounded by the forests of two national parks. Newly-shorn sheep and nestling ponds dotted the paddocks which were punctuated by the stark, silver statues of giant karri* trunks, their dead limbs lifted like supplicants to the sky.

The morning after we arrived at Tingledale, we followed the farm's dog and the trail signs across the paddocks and fence stiles into the Valley of the Giants National Park. In the warm, filtered sun, hundreds of tall karris gleamed, their silver-gray trunks reaching as high as 150 feet before the first branch broke the perfect symmetry. Growing to heights of 250 feet or more, they were impossible to capture on camera. How I wished I could somehow share their grandeur with those who have no idea that eucalypts can grow as immense as redwoods.

Back on the coastal highway, we hurried on to Denmark and its famous bakery. Denmark earned its name well, set amidst rolling hills and dales, with streets curving down toward the Denmark River. The river looked Danish, too, bordered by a parkland of wide lawns and bright flowers under burgeoning gums. Three or four little dingy boats nestled in the tea colored water under a white wooden bridge. Saturday afternoon strollers and seagulls grouped themselves colorfully about the wooden tables and benches or clustered in gazebos, eating bakery treats and take-out goodies.

Our youth hostel informant proved right: the bakery was equal to the standards of any Danish bakery. Like children we oohed and ahhed as we inhaled the fragrant aromas and ogled the tempting trays of opulent items. After making several choices of sinful delicacies we took them outside to eat in the sun by the riverbank. And then we returned to buy some more.

Sometimes I would catch my reflection in a window and noted, yes, slightly thicker--and not likely to return to svelter days. Amazingly, I wasn't devastated. I was enjoying our way of eating a few treats, some take-outs, fish and chips, bakery goodies and deserts. I was happy and healthy and was at last accepting the fact that a woman's worth is not measured by the width of her waist.

Approaching Albany--only a few kilometers from Denmark --we could hardly believe that only a week before we'd withered in the heat and flies of Wittenoom. The dust and heat and bareness of the north seemed worlds and years removed from this cool, green, coastal landscape. We had no idea what to expect in Albany, no idea what kind of people we would soon be meeting or what sort of houses we'd be living in. One thing was sure, we looked forward to the new places where at last we could spread out, organize weeks of accumulated car clutter, and spend some time getting involved in one community. We felt as if we were dancing lightly forward into a new cycle, one which promised to be very right and wonderful.

Trees like tethered balloons.

ALBANY

I HAD SPECIAL memories of my first visit to Albany. In the summer of 1969, I arrived there with my school teacher friend, Kaylene, after hitchhiking across the continent on what were then mostly dirt roads. Our ride had dropped us at Albany's resort/beach area of Emu Point. From there, Kaylene and I walked along a lovely tree-shaded road and surveyed the residences much as we'd done in other towns. Picking a house that looked like it contained friendly people, we rang the bell. An older man and woman answered the door. We explained who we were and asked if we could throw our sleeping bags on their back lawn for the night since we were hesitant to sleep on the beach.

Immediately, we were ushered inside, invited to stay in their guest room, offered hot showers and given a warm meal. We stayed three days with Mr. and Mrs. Hastings, enjoying their hospitality and companionship. These generous people even took us on tours of the area. Each morning I strolled across their backyard to the long strip of white beach where I'd swim in the warm turquoise water--never dreaming that one day I'd return to that spot with my husband.

Twenty summers later, under heavy grey skies, Sid and I entered Albany--both a little snappy from the cold and the many days of driving. It was good to know this would be the last night of youth hostels and carting and unpacking and repacking gear.

In the late afternoon, we drove to Little Grove, a tiny, but budding community a few minutes drive along the bay from Albany, and located the MacFarland's house. We introduced ourselves to the family--Jo, Don and baby Rossalyn--who were about to trust us with their home. We were pleased to find that we got along well with these people whom till now we'd only met via long distance phone calls.

Jo and Don both worked in agriculture--he had a position with the AG Department, and she was finishing her Ph.D. Jo confided that she was expecting to spend most of her Christmas holidays in the university library in Perth devouring books and materials that were unavailable in remote Albany.

The house was a sleek new red brick structure with a corrugated metal roof curving in bullnose style over wide brick verandahs. We could understand why Jo and Don were eager to find a house sitter. They were avid gardeners and environmentalists, and besides the large lawns and flower beds there were several sandy areas where newly planted native seedlings were starting to take root.

We toured the spacious and tastefully modern interior--the master bedroom with its king size bed; the office where we all paused to exchange computer jargon; the comfortable lounge and dining rooms and the shiny brick and wood kitchen where our eyes lit up when we saw the microwave. After a bit of coaxing from Sid, the MacFarlands managed to come up with a list of electrical projects for him to do while we stayed in their home.

Across the street from the house, the trees and shrubs were just high enough to obscure the view of the bay. However, from the bay front road, a stone's throw away, one could look directly across Princess Royal Harbor to Albany, or east toward the massive headlands that obscured the open sea.

Albany and it environs offered a varied display of terrain and extraordinary landscapes. Off-shore islands sprawled hither and thither. Some were pancake-shaped and colored, while others lay like sleeping dogs, grey and heavy. Hulking heads rose majestically near the curving harbor entrance. Wavy, grey-green hills rimmed the bays, edged with a thin frill where white, sandy beaches separated them from the sea. North of Albany, the shadowy forms of the nearby Porongurup and Stirling Ranges shimmered jagged on the horizon.

If one looked down on a map of the area, the water would look like a lopsided kidney. To the left ballooned Princess Royal Harbor with Albany situated to the north and Little Grove to the south. The tidal action left a swath of grey mud flats where pelicans and black swans strolled or swam depending on the time of day. These pelicans were not the grubby gray California kind, but appeared to be of the English butler variety--aristocratically looking down beaks that rested on their chests as they lumbered about in brilliant white shirt fronts and black tails.

Princess Royal Harbor was in effect a bay within a bay, split off from the larger harbor of King George Sound to the east by a large spit, (or a small peninsula) across which whipping winds frequently raced. The harbor was so well protected that the water hardly blinked as the winds skimmed over its surface. Even in the vivid indigo and aqua waters of King George Sound the waves scuttled like perky ponies rather than wild stallions, galloping ahead of the wind. It was there that the lovely beach and rocky slopes of Frenchman Bay posed like a picture postcard. On wind-free days Sid and I liked to eat our breakfast there, high on a ledge of rusty rock looking down at the unbelievably clear water. Here, too, crumbled a jumble of bricks--the remains of the old Norwegian whaling station.

Albany itself sprawled seaward between and around the base of two largish hills aspiringly named Mt. Melville and Mt. Clarence. York, the main street, ran from the Albany Highway, and Perth, right down to the water. As Western Australia's earliest settlement, Albany benefited from the old stone edifices characteristic of the 19th century British buildings. What added a unique and picturesque flavor to Albany were the rocks. Besides Mounts Clarence and Melville, which were slabs of solid grey rock broken by spurts of scrub, boulders the size of houses, box cars or automobiles protruded from lawns and shopping centers or alongside roads and residences. Some homes even rose right out of the rock.

Sid and I loved settling into a house and an established routine. We explored the town and the surrounding area and hunkered down to work at our computers for several hours a day. Thanks to the lady at the local bookshop, I located a woman who kindly loaned me a guitar, and I enjoyed practicing daily. Everyday we took some time out for exercise. Besides biking and walking around Little Grove, I delighted in Albany's modern aquatic center, the nearby tennis courts and the local fitness club. Through these facilities, I participated in aerobics, squash and tennis games with the local mothers.

On the rare windless days, Sid and I biked along the narrow road following the curves of the Little Grove beach front. Our walks frequently turned into Olympic workouts as we strained against the maddening wind. No matter which direction we were heading, it was wrong. On leaving the house we'd think, well, at least when we return the wind will be in our favor. But it wasn't! It blew so hard and was so fickle, that it was enough to make us ponder serious issues--like how did bugs cling to leaves? Why weren't the flies all blown away, and how could birds reproduce?

Albany from Mt. Melville.

CHRISTMAS DOWN UNDER

AROUND MID-DECEMBER we noticed the first signs of Christmas appearing in Albany. The locals treated it almost as an afterthought, probably because it was sandwiched in the middle of another holy event, the summer holidays.* As far as Sid and I were concerned, Christmas seemed somewhat remote because we had not yet established a circle of local friends.

In early December some sparse decorations sprinkled shop shelves, and two weeks before Christmas stores or banks went all out with a few strips of tinsel here or a sparkly, glittery thing there. Woolworths, while devoting a meager half aisle to Christmas supplies, loaded four aisles with pretty tins and boxes of candy and biscuits and Christmas cakes*. These Aussies had their priorities in order.

Now and again we'd catch a glimpse of a small decorated tree hiding behind someone's living room window. It's unlikely that these were live trees since evergreens are too scarce and too precious to cut down. The main street displayed Albany's only outdoor decorations--strings of red, yellow, blue, and green globes which were festively illuminated at night. It seemed right not to have traditional northern trimmings gushing all over the place. Frosted evergreens and holly berries would look ridiculous in such a warm, dry and summery place.

Even though our own Christmas was low-key, I knew that there were plenty of holiday festivities going on behind Albany's undecorated doors. Simultaneously with family gatherings and business parties, I knew that the schools were busily drawing to the end of the year with exams, graduations and parties. I remembered when I taught school in Keith how those days had been tremendously social times. There were dinners out, treats were sent to school by parents nearly every day, and routine affairs were conducted in an atmosphere of fun and freedom.

I knew, too, that many Australian families would celebrate much as I had done in 1967 at "Stirling" with Diana's first husband's family. All dressed up, we had exchanged gifts and drank exquisite champagne from crystal glasses. In the afternoon we sat down to a flower-bedecked formal table laden with traditional turkey and Christmas pudding. The rest of the day was spent lounging around the swimming pool in 95 degree weather.

And there were those people who would load up the entire family in their station wagon or motor home and take off on their summer vacations to caravan parks or resorts. Like Katherine's family in Perth, they would completely dispense with traditional dinners, opting instead to pack a picnic lunch to eat in a park or on a beach.

Sid and I brought in from our verandah a perfect, little potted cedar-like tree and adorned it with masses of red, white, gold and green curled ribbon streamers and wrapping paper cones. The tree glorified our living room like a dazzlingly dressed gnome. Not bad for four dollars worth of paper and ribbon. Beneath it, Peter Panda* and a red-scarfed and hatted polar bear borrowed from baby Rossalyn's room, presided amidst a jumble of colorful packages.

On the evening of December 23, we drove to Middleton Beach to partake in a uniquely Australian tradition called "Carols by Candlelight." Throughout Australia, community clubs put on the event which, as far as I knew, was always held outdoors.

At the carol site we climbed up the grass and stone tiers of a hillside that rose from the sandy beach and lapping waters of Allen Cove. As the night descended, throngs of people gathered, each one bearing a booklet of carols and a white candle in a cardboard holder. Gradually the hillside became a sea of families sitting on blankets, beach chairs and atop the stone embankments.

At the base of the slope a stage housed an acoustics system, the Salvation Army band, a group of bright blue-clad choir children and a master of ceremonies. The band was unique. So immersed in their music were the musicians that they frequently failed to notice when a song was finished and continued on with a rousing couple of measures before realizing that the last verse had been sung.

Children hurried to ignite their candles, while others chose to wait. It was tricky balancing carol books while protecting the candles from the wind. A frequently employed tactic for sheltering the flame was to crimp the edges of the cardboard square up around the candle. A little boy in front of us forgot to pay attention to his candle and managed to set aflame both his cardboard holder and an

A happy Christmas in Albany.

adjacent tree. His frantic parents, laughing with embarrassment, doused the flames with handfuls of dirt and splashes of coca cola.

As we sang a carol called *Little Donkey*, I turned and looked behind us. Yellow flames pinpricked the hillside softly suffusing the landscape of faces with orange light. Some people protected their flickering flames with their hands, which took on an orange glow. Overhead the stars glittered through the silhouetted branches of Norfolk Island pines. In the water the dark shape of a sailboat with several lighted candles gently rose and fell with the waves. Below us, the wide, white collars of the choir children fluttered precariously close to their lighted candles.

Our Christmas Day Down Under was low-key and pleasant. It was the first Christmas that Sid and I had been alone--just the two of us. For once, the day was bright and warm, with nearly no wind. We opened our presents in the bright shafts of sunlight smiling through the windows burnishing the multi-colors of our patchwork tree and the growing piles of paper.

After a British breakfast of crumpets, Americanized by being whole wheat, we set off in the car for Emu Point, the beach area where caravan parks abounded and tourists thronged during the holidays. On this sunny Christmas morning, groups of swimmers and sunbathers already sprinkled the sand. The clear shallow water gleamed turquoise. Beyond, the deep water glistened velvet indigo. Three iron-red freighters were anchored out in the sound--hulking contrasts to the rocky-slabbed outcrops of cliffs and islands and sand spits.

As we walked and jogged the length of the wide beach, a shell caught my eye. It was bright orange imprinted with a yellow paisley pattern. Picking it up, I held it to the sun. What a beautiful candle holder or night light it would make. Soon, for the first time, I was noticing one by one, the acres of shells we were carelessly walking across--purple and magenta and pinks and roses. I remembered the statement about art mimicking nature. From some shells must derive the shape of Japanese fans, and certain colors must inspire the delicacy of Japanese prints. Before long I was pottering along the beach, bending over every few steps to collect shells--something I once would have disdained as a pastime reserved for children and old ladies. I procured a plastic bag from a nearby kiosk, where the proprietor said that he kept bags on hand to supply the shell collectors. Outfitted now for complete indulgence, I collected my Christmas gifts from the sea all the way back to Emu Point.

Emu Point jutted out into the sound nearly meeting the rocks of the shore across from it, forming a protected little inner bay. We had walked along the beach on the outer side of the sound. Now, we returned to the inner side of the point and joined the other holiday makers sunning on the beach. Adjoining the strip of sand, three grassy terraces rose up to a tree-lined lawn area containing a parking lot, a deli and an attractive restaurant crammed with fancy folks sitting at tables laden with wine bottles in ice buckets.

We enjoyed being part of the outdoor groups, the clusters of picnickers, swimmers and ball chasers and little ladies in wide hats. We joined them on the beach with our own Christmas picnic, a

75

delicious indulgence of local fish and chips. Albany had poured out her best for a sparkling Christmas Day, one of the few clear, calm days we'd experienced. How lucky we felt, basking in the warmth of the Aussie sun, celebrating the holiday in the laid-back, outdoor Aussie way.

MIDDLE AGED SURFIES

ALL TOO SOON the day came when we raced around the Little
Grove house slicking it up, gathering and packing our gear in
readiness to leave. I enjoyed the cleaning. It was satisfying to see the
place shiny and sleek, with bright flowers and fresh sheets and
fragrant new soaps in their holders. I imagined how I would delight
in returning to a polished house and wanted to give that delight to Jo
and Don.

With our gear tossed loosely into the car, we drove to the other
side of Albany to begin Phase Two of our house-sitting situation.
The house on Lindfield Crescent belonged to Ian Hereford, a friend
of the MacFarlands. He worked at the Department of Conservation
and Land Management. Originally we were going to Albany to
house-sit for Ian, but when he told Jo and Don about us, they had
asked if we would also take care of their place.

The timing turned out to be perfect. Ian left town a week before Jo
and Don returned, so there was an overlap of houses for that time.
During that week, Sid moved into Ian's house while I stayed at the
Little Grove house. We each luxuriated in the chance to savor some
quiet time alone.

Ian's square brick house sat with its back to the ocean which was
just a couple of kilometers away. It was built on a site high enough
above its steep driveway and long flight of stairs to afford a
commanding view of yellow farm fields and bands of grey green
trees. While it was not as modern or as pretty as the Little Grove
place, Ian's house with its big windows and minimal overhang,
opened itself to the warmth of light and air and seemed bright and
spacious.

Sid and I quickly established a routine of driving to Emu Point or
Middleton Beach every day, no matter how windy, to walk or to
surf. I had discovered surfing--and I loved it. In the past, my style
would have been to sedately swim parallel to the shore atop the
undulating roofs of waves. But now I delighted in joining them in
their roiling shoreward dance.

A long green curl would gallop toward us. Just before it broke,

Sid, looking over his shoulder, would dive and then be carried along like a torpedo. Imitating his stance and timing, I too, would then shoot beachward on the laughing fingers of spewing foam.

"Yeah! Wow!" we'd shout, picking ourselves up from the shore and splashing back through the knee-deep swirls for more. Sid bright-eyed, would be laughing and exuberantly dunking and diving with unrestrained glee. I'd never seen him so "there".

Sometimes instead of surfing, I would float lightly and effortlessly aloft with the tilt of the waves. Other times, as the rows of waves charged upon us, we'd turn around to stand and let the deep green wall break over our backs, spraying and splintering into white foam.

The waves were best if just large enough either to plunge under or be carried upon them, but not so big as to throttle and frighten. At Middleton Beach the water was warm enough and the waves small enough to be friendly. Children floated and bobbed atop and among the heaving waves even further out than we were. When a big wave swelled, curling into a green cavity, little heads and limbs would protrude like pimentos from a stuffed olive.

People spend fabulous sums to be pummeled and pounded by masseurs and machines, yet tumbling with the waves invigorated me beyond those forms of therapy. As the water splashed over and around me, pummeling and vibrating my back, it seemed the aeration lifted and lightened me along with it.

It had been years since I'd played in the surf. Discovering the surf anew at middle-age brought me into a new relationship with it. There was no winning or losing, no teamwork or rules--just float and bob and dunk and fling myself ahead of the rollicking waves, and straddle up in the swirling foam to wade back to the next regiment clustering one atop the other.

Our days of beach walking and surfing, however, were coming to an end with the approach of January 14th and Ian's return to Albany. With mixed feelings, Sid and I readied ourselves to pack up and move on. We had grown to love Albany and the area, and had enjoyed our private residences, participating in the community and making new friends. But we also were eager to start the big push across the continent to the east. And, we had something special to look forward to on the day of our departure.

Throughout the southwest, I'd seen posters advertising the sailing vessel, *Leeuwin II*. I'd always wanted to sail on a "tall ship" with masses of canvas romantically speeding us ahead of the wind. One day in early December, I had wandered into Albany's tourist bureau and was thrilled to discover that the *Leeuwin* was coming to Albany. I had immediately bought our special Christmas presents--two tickets for the *Leeuwin's* morning cruise on January 14th. We would be leaving Albany on a high and romantic note.

"Hanging out" on Ian's clothesline.

THE ROMANTIC *LEEUWIN* II

UNDER A SOGGY shroud of morning mist Albany's cement docks gleamed grayly in the Sunday stillness. Calling gulls hovered and dived above the silver sea, then rose high to rest upon the network of cranes and silos towering in the chill salt air. At the far end of the dock a hulking freighter scowled as busy cranes lifted cargo from her black hold onto waiting trucks. Dusted on this vision of twentieth century commerce, the masts and rigging of the *Leeuwin II* rose like a creamy cobweb, a valiant reminder of another era.

Sid and I crossed the gangplank into *Leeuwin's* colorful world of raincoated passengers intermingling with a blue-clad crew. These men and women, young *and* old, scurried and climbed happily about, frequently stopping to cluster into pairs or groups hugging and chattering in obvious delight.

Drizzle still dampened *Leeuwin's* decks as with a thrill of expectation her engines roared and she was underway. A teenage girl in pink and chartreuse neon hair bands commanded the wheel, her sturdy tan legs in their cut-off jeans planted firmly apart. Standing casually available next to her, wearing brilliant white shorts and a black pullover with golden epaulets, was the first mate. To the side strode the captain, in pressed black trousers, crisp white shirt with gleaming epaulets and black commander's cap. As the voyage proceeded and we learned more about our crew, we came to admire this man and his apparent calm.

Under our youthful helmswoman's hand, the *Leeuwin* chugged along the channel leading towards the outer bay of King George Sound. I was so engrossed in the deck activities that I was surprised to look up and see that the rigging ropes overhead were colorfully pinpricked with clambering crew members. The two lower-most crossbeams looked like a roosting place for a bevy of very large spidery birds. On the next beam up, in diverse attire, perched eight more climbers, and even higher up a final twosome clung like burrs to the swaying crow's nest.

With bodies draped over the large spars, the crew members inched sideways along the swaying mast rope like highwire artists, legs spread wide, depressing the rope in a deep V. Although they were snapped on to the rigging by a belt harness, the sensation at that shimmying height must have been one of great vulnerability. Arriving at their stations, still draping over the beam, they then set about busily untying the many loops of rope binding the sails in place. After time and patient effort, the sails slowly loosened, slithering lazily to form baggy pockets fluttering below the crew.

I remembered a workshop I'd once participated in. Each of us, wearing a harness, had climbed a rope ladder high into a tree and then crossed hand over hand on a stretched rope to a second tree. We snapped our harness to the overhead rope, which also had been attached to a rope controlled by the facilitator on the ground. On completion of the exercise he could lower us to earth, slowly or fast, depending on our request. I had asked to be lowered fast, and shot exhilaratingly toward the ground. That seminar was called *Transforming Fear* and now I felt tremendous respect for the young crew who were draped precariously across the swaying beams high above the bucking boat. Their radiant faces reflected a similar exhilaration.

Slowly the climbers inched back down the riggings to the deck, and then it was time to open the sails. Several groups of crew members, with passengers encouraged to join in, gathered at appointed stations and on signal vigorously hauled on lines. Gradually the countless canopies of canvas sprang into life and the three masts strained with bulging sails. The engines were cut. Leeuwin was under the power of the wind.

I'd imagined that this moment would be romantic, transcending the fumes and clatter of our motorized century for the silent purity of wind and another age. But it didn't happen that way. *Leeuwin* didn't skim, and neither did she shoot gracefully forward. She continued her bucking motions plunging deeply into troughs of waves and lumbering skyward acrest them. Our ears were deafened by the noise of the rushing wind. *Leeuwin* was slow. Had I been considering sailing, say, to England, it would take *months*. Any hankerings I might have had to relive the romantic days of transoceanic clipper cruises dissolved a little more each time *Leeuwin* wallowed in and out of another trough.

Leeuwin's crewmembers performing their highwire act.

Once we were cruising, morning tea was announced, and I bounded down the steep hatch stairway to gather a handful of biscuits* to munch. Over the loudspeaker I heard a dialogue explaining the *Leeuwin* and her crew. STS (Sail Training Ship) *Leeuwin II* was a barquentine designed along traditional lines and built in 1986. She was conceived and dedicated to the idea of offering people of all ages a place in which to develop self-esteem, discipline, teamwork, leadership, independence and initiative. She takes on as many as 40 crew members and for a fee of $870 one can learn the art of sailing on a ten-day training cruise. She also circumnavigates Australia taking on passengers. Fifty people on a half day cruise, at $40 each, helps to finance her upkeep.

A crew member explained to me that many of today's crew had done the ten-day training in the past. Now every time *Leeuwin* calls into Albany, they can come down and crew for half a day. That explained why there was so much greeting and hugging going on among the crew at the start of the trip, like a family reunion.

At one point, as *Leeuwin* progressed toward the massive grey headlands, the Captain barked the command, "Stand by to tack." Calls and shouts flew from stern to bow, and the crew scurried to man the ropes. To my unschooled eyes it seemed to take a long time for this flurry of activity to elicit results. The captain strode left and right and then forward of the current helmswoman, a freckled girl in a purple track suit intently screwing up her face and whirling the helm like a roulette wheel. He shouted instructions, or simply stood, arms crossed, with one hand at his chin, observing. As *Leeuwin* finally shuddered into position and the fluttering sails at last took up wind, the captain muttered as he passed by us, "That's what you call a backward tack."

I had great respect for this man willing to set sail with an amateur crew and a load of ignorant passengers. He must have had a very understanding personality and been highly regarded, too, as he'd also been roundly hugged by the returning crew.

A happy, gay atmosphere prevailed aboard Leeuwin, with lots of laughing and joking and smiling. I detected no sense of worry or concern on anyone's part, not even when water splashed over our decks while tacking "backwards", and the ship dipped and hovered sideways over the sea. Some of the crew were watch leaders who had a good deal of experience and seemed capable of instructing others. One curvacious blond lady, the only other person with epaulets on her uniform, seemed to be the second in command. She scurried to and fro across the bow while the captain held forth from the stern. He'd shout instructions and then she'd take over, directing and commanding with much assurance.

Sid and I had both been struck by the casual Aussie attitude toward safety, finding it very refreshing that people are allowed to take responsibility for themselves. In Broome, for example, the long jetty had a narrow ledge circumventing its edge forty feet above the water. People clambered down the ladder from the jetty and casually walked, cast lines, hauled in fish, or lounged on this narrow bridge. There were no warning signs posted, nor rails to keep people from falling. At the Blow Hole and the Natural Bridge in Albany, signs warned people that they would proceed at their own risk. That's all. No handrails cut one off from walking where one wanted. One was expected to use one's own judgment and be responsible. I suspect that this happy state of affairs exists because Australia's legal system does not operate (as yet) by the same lawsuit mentality as it does in the United States.

At any rate, throughout the course of our *Leeuwin* cruise, never once was there mentioned anything that had to do with safety. No cautions about where to stand or what to do if one fell overboard. No evacuation instructions. No designation of life jackets. Several big drum-shaped cylinders bolted with big hooks to the deck, bore inscriptions that said: IN CASE OF DROWNING THROW OVERBOARD AND INFLATE, and left me wondering how I'd unbolt them. Like everyone else aboard, I assumed that someone was in control and knew what they were doing, and that all was expected to go well.

After another hour's tacking first toward the heads and then back toward Middleton Beach, the captain shouted the command, "Crank her up!" as the sails came down. Once again the agile crew scampered skyward to perform their dazzling aerial act. Slowly, bit by bit, each sail became mere formless canvas, which was painstakingly rolled up and tied down by the covey of high roosting crew.

As we docked, the steward announced over the loud speaker, "*Leeuwin* will be leaving tomorrow for a ten-day training cruise. Thirty people have already signed up." In his most tempting tone, he added, "We still have room for ten more."

Sid and I exchanged speculative looks. I loved the *idea* of it. What a lot I'd learn. I, too, could dangle 50 feet in the air over a swaying ship. I, too, could learn to tie knots and heave lines and maybe even share hugs with the captain. Twenty years ago, I'd have leapt at following that romantic notion. Today the *idea* was lovely and it was enough. My head was dizzy from the morning's short ride. I knew that I didn't want to toss about in a tiny bunk in a claustrophobic cabin. I knew I could be satisfied with the morning's experience and appreciate the happy fate that landed me in a century when I could satisfy my wanderlust by crossing the ocean in comfort, rather than in queasy months of rolling and rocking on a tiny ship.

Later that afternoon, before leaving Albany, Sid and I drove along the harbor cliffs hoping to see the *Leeuwin* plying her afternoon tour. Sure enough there she was. It was well beyond an hour since she'd left port and, as I'd expected, her sails were not yet up. I could imagine the tight rope dance being performed at that moment above her decks. From this distance she looked no bigger than my thumbnail, a dark speck under a tiny web of crisscrossed lines. And it was then that I fell in love with her, so vulnerable and gallant amidst the endless blue basin of the sea. Separated from the reality of those swaying decks, I could see her again as the fulfillment of my illusions. She was utterly, beautifully romantic.

THE STIRLINGS

AFTER SEEING LEEUWIN off, Sid and I said goodbye to Albany and our lovely house and turned our car northward. Instead of heading straight to the east, we had decided that before we left Western Australia we wanted to spend a few days in the Buddhist Monastery which we'd visited while staying with the Pereys. So we headed north toward Perth, with the Stirling Ranges 80 km away, as our destination for the first night on the road.

The attractive rural road was bordered by little farms with shady trees and sheep or goats and colorful flowers dotting golden fields and green gardens. I was grateful to be here amidst this freshness and pastoral beauty. Yet my enjoyment was tinged with sadness--because I knew it would change. Just as the charming countryside of California and the peaceful farmlands in other states had fallen under the hatchets of developers and pollution, this place would too. Inevitably, pretty places attract people, and developers are always ready to accommodate them by leveling the forests and fields, by strewing them with suburbs and destroying the character of the land which had originally attracted them.

After half an hour's drive, the rolling hills with their tiny farms gave way to wide open farmland, yellow with ripening grain, and offset by the grey-green scrubby hillsides of the Porongurup Ranges. As we drove the next 40 km, the Stirling Ranges loomed directly ahead of us, dancing in and out of our view in ever-changing shapes and shades of blue. Another half an hour found us in the heart of the Stirling Range National Park looking at the mighty, jagged ridges silhouetted like cardboard cutouts against the sundown sky.

We pulled into the only sign of human habitation--the Stirling Range Caravan Park. This was the slow season--most people don't visit the inland parks during the heat of summer--so we needn't have bothered to book ahead. For $7 each, we had our choice of the several attractive bungalows which the caravan park reserved for youth hostelers.

The next day was a landmark day as I exalted in discovering how far my body had come in renewing itself. We climbed Bluff Knoll--

one of the mighty captains of the Stirling Ranges. It was exercise such as I love and used to long for. It was strenuous, sweaty and tiring, and we sank exhausted and hot into our car on our return to the parking lot. I could hardly believe that there had been a time, not long ago, when just to climb my house stairs had been an undertaking fraught with frustration and dismay.

That night after dinner I walked across the nearby sundown shadowed field watching the roos feeding, and noticed--nothing. Not an ache or pain or stiffness, not one residue of the morning's outing. That really told me how much I had improved. In the past I had paid dearly for my forays into attempted exercise. The shakiness and achiness would ooze throughout my hips and legs. But on this day I felt nothing!

As we climbed that morning, Sid walked slowly to compliment my pace. I plugged along, one small step up at a time, and reached the top of the bluff in just over two hours. We climbed through a dense growth of shrubby gums and grey-green brush punctuated here and there by the scarlet flare of bottle brush. The yellow, then gold, then dark core of banksia* candles told their story of youth, maturity and decay. As we climbed higher, the view to the west became ever more magnificent and the slopes ever more jagged and Alpine.

From the crest, the scalloped slopes of the Stirlings slid like sculpted shadows ever dimmer toward the western horizon. Below and between the ranges, the grey-green scrub formed a dense forest of leaves and limbs. It looked like pictures I've seen of Africa-- sweeping brush, grey twiggy trees, ethereal peaks of ranges dwindling into the hazy distance.

Once we'd ascended beyond the sea of trees, the rocky path wound upward through mountainous terrain. Bright pink tea trees, bonsaied by wind and rock and climate, clustered like mountain heather. Coarse green, wind-cropped shrubs lined the granite trail. From the top we could see the tiny circle of the parking lot below, with its entry road ribboning to a shred in the distance where lay our caravan park and the main highway. Beyond the sloping skirts of the forest, oceans of yellow grasslands stretched on all sides. We could see the Porongurup Range barely visible in haze 40 km to the south,

The view from Bluff Knoll, the Stirlings.

and beyond them the horizon was a dark heavy gray, indicating that Albany wallowed in its typical coastal cold weather.

The descent was difficult but bearable, with the steep trail frequently consisting of dirt stair steps shored up by spikes and boards. All the way down I had to use my knees as brakes in order not to slip on the loose rocks and dirt. We rested often. I took it slowly and managed well, although my legs felt shaky and unsteady. As we'd climbed, I'd been saying to myself...*Next Mt. Fuji, then Kilamanjaro, the Great Wall, the Milford Track...so many other heights I will achieve.* As I descended, I reminded myself of those goals, but added to my images...*I am a goat...a sure-footed springy mountain goat bounding gracefully and agilely downhill.* It worked!

Back at the cabin, it was wonderful to collapse on a chair, hot, sticky, tired, but elated. Later, at the pool I grew even more pleased as I chatted to two girl hitchhikers we'd driven to the trail head. These young things said that they were really wiped out after their hike, and that their legs felt like jelly. That disclosure gladdened me, for I was no different than those two girls. How far I'd come!

As if to round out the specialness of that day, there had been the mother roo who had appeared just as we approached the trail head that morning. After the two young girls had proceeded on ahead, she materialized out of nowhere, like an ethereal vision just for us alone.

Feeding rice cakes to the mother roo.

She was a delicate creature, with soft, trusting eyes and from her pouch protruded the curious little face and four legs of a large joey.

The little mother eagerly accepted from my hands the rice cakes and rye crackers I held out to her. As the area was blazing hot with no sign of water for miles, Sid suggested that she might like some water and poured a bit from our canteen into my cupped hands. Daintily she dipped her head and quickly lapped up the water, and repeatedly drank each time Sid poured out more water into my hands.

Running out of rice cakes, we crossed the parking lot back to the car and were amazed to turn around and see the little mother hopping right along behind us. After she had delicately drunk down more water and accepted more rice cakes into her hand-like paws, we knew we could not delay any longer and must embark on our climb before the day grew any hotter. We reluctantly pulled ourselves away, proceeding up the trail. After a few steps, I turned around. The mother roo had disappeared, and I was left with the feeling that her presence had somehow been a gift, something special for us alone. How I hoped that the trust she had offered us would never be abused.

*   *   *

After two more days of rugged hiking and enjoying our comfortable cabins, we left the Stirlings for Serpentine near Perth, and for our retreat at the Bodhinyana Monastery.

THE MONASTERY AND I

I SAT ON the cushioned folding chair which straddled the crest of the hill in front of my nun's kuti (hut). All around me slender trunked gums gleamed silver white. Yellow grasses, heathery shrubs and orange sprays of Christmas tree blossoms shimmered in the occasional breeze. The green fountainy spikes of blackboys* squatted like haystacks on the ground or perched high atop black-burnt zigzag trunks. Below, the broad coastal plain unfolded like a checkered grey-green and yellow cloth blending into a pale blue hazy line where the land met the unseen sea. Savoring the view, I reviewed my last three days, with Sid, at the Bodhinyana Monastery, and some answers came to the question: Why am I here?

That first night when Rolf, the white-clad Scots novitiate, led me up the isolated trail and deposited me at my kuti, I was delighted. I had always wanted my own self-contained little hideaway where I could soak up solitude and silence without interruption. A door and two windows peered from the front of the white board hut, sheltered by a tin roof extending over a miniature brick porch. A third, south-facing window, was shaded by a fine black mesh awning, and abutting the northern wall was a small tin rain tank. The kuti's one room was just big enough for me to lay out my sleeping bag, clothes and books on a thin foam pad. In one corner of the floor clustered the only materials provided to guests of the monastery. There were a candle, matches, a couple of carved Buddhas, some sticks of incense, water jug, Kleenex, and an enamel bowl.

Sundown had painted its fading light on the yellow brick and wrought iron entry gates when Sid and I arrived. We had stopped along the way to load up with fruits and vegetables to bring as offerings, and ate up our last bites of food; we would be fasting until noon the next day.

We just had time to chat a bit with the abbot and to ferry bedding to our separate huts before 6:50 when the bells called us to evening meditation. The abbot knew that we had no Buddhist training. I had told him that my interest lay not in the formal teachings of Buddhism, but I yearned to spend some time in the monastery's atmosphere of devotions and discipline. The abbot suggested that I not wear shorts and asked us not to approach a monk with conversation or to engage in idle chitchat. I'd already been cautioned by friends not to touch a monk.

Inside the attractive brick temple, round black cushions and glass water bottles were distributed on plush rose-colored carpet. To honor their customs, Sid and I followed the examples of the monks and other visitors, and kneeled and bowed three times to the huge polished wooden Buddha at the front altar. Then, settling into a crossed-legged position on our cushions, we dropped our hands in our laps and closed our eyes to sit silently for the next hour.

The abbot sat on the largest cushion facing frontward. In the first row sat four saffron-robed monks. Behind them were two white-clad novitiates followed by two male visitors, then Sid and me. Employing several leg shifts, I made it through the hour of meditation which was followed by several minutes of chanting. Then a tape came on the loud speaker. We sat on the floor for another hour listening to a famous teacher discuss conditional and unconditional mind and the difficulty of transcending the body's continual demands and limitations. It was certainly an apt topic as I struggled to sit quietly with numb buttocks, tingling legs, pinched knees and buckled blood vessels.

When we finally stepped out of the hall into the velvet night, we were greeted by a dazzling fireworks display of stars. I'd loved the exquisite silence of the meditation, but this--ah! Although I was tired and sticky, I passed up the shower I longed for. It was ten o'clock and we'd be rising at four in the morning. Sleep seemed more important than cleanliness.

The morning meditations proceeded much like the ones practiced at night. We meditated for one hour and chanted for half an hour. We were then free to leave the temple to walk on the grounds or meditate for another hour. After that, we gathered for a morning drink of tea or milo* (with plenty of caffeine, sugar and milk, all of which I avoid) and were assigned our daily work.

Monks hitched up their robes or donned overalls and scattered to tractors and construction sites, cement and gravel piles. The abbot gave me the task of sweeping the maze of outdoor stairs and walks.

I took my time sweeping. I had to, the broom was so thin and sparse. The novitiate, Rolf, had jokingly suggested that I meditate on the cosmic meaning of each leaf. But it wasn't the leaves so much as the flagstones that drew me. I found I liked the stones' pure-swept beauty. Each revealed shiny pink and salmon streaks, glints of green and silvery tones. Unadulterated, uninterrupted stonework. So pure.

While I swept I thought, "I'm here to put the body and desires into perspective." Sweep. "I'm waiting for that midday meal and there's nothing to do but wait." Sweep. "Let it go." Sweep. "In this setting I get to notice and confront and, hopefully, transcend: Those desirous parts of myself *(When can I eat?)*." Sweep. "The fearful parts *(What if I don't get enough to eat?)*." Sweep. "The distraction parts *(I must shift my numb crossed legs)*." Sweep. "The appearance- focused part *(I look washed-out without lipstick)*." Sweep. "The impatient part *(Can I wait until tomorrow before I eat again?)*." Sweep.

Finally it was ten-thirty and we went to the eating room. Water jugs, bowls, mugs, knives and Chinese soup spoons were grouped along wide carpet runners lining three walls. A batik cloth laden with platters and bowls of food was spread on the floor in the middle of the room. The monks sat silently along the runners in descending order. There were also two attractive white-clad women who had delivered food that morning in their white car.

These two came to the monastery once a week and seemed quite at home. After several moments of chanting and silence, at the abbot's indication the women moved forward on their knees, bowed, and began passing platters of food to the abbot. He helped himself and then passed them to the second in command and on down the line. Every time a bowl was passed on, the receiver and giver pressed their palms together and bowed silently.

Bowing was a big part of the ritual. Whenever anyone entered or left the temple or eating room, he or she knelt and bowed three times to the resident Buddha.

My bowl was still half full when a tray of tea kettles was passed around and each monk filled his mug. I looked at Leo, one of the retreatants, and signaled, "Am I supposed to stop eating?" He indicated that I could eat until the abbot finished his tea. Since I was still hungry, I hurriedly crammed in as much food as I could in the few minutes left.

Prior to coming to the monastery, we'd been told that the monks must eat everything they put in their bowls. They must gage their servings so they were not stuffed, yet not leave hungry. However, I did notice that three men (more enlightened?) set full bowls aside long before the stop-eating signal had been given, and I wondered about it.

After the meal, talking was resumed and people scattered to make use of their afternoon free time. I resumed sweeping, but the going was slow as monks approached me and began conversations. One monk told me that some visitors to the monastery fit right in while others would disrupt and be a drain on the monks.

Another monk, Venerable Simi, explained to me how monks, when approaching one another, always maintain a prayerful pose. In the presence of a higher ranked monk, they must keep their heads lower than that of their superior. He admitted that this was tricky at times. The best a tall monk could do was to hunch down in a futile gesture of shrinking when encountering a shorter, senior monk.

I understood the reason for these age-old formalities. They were designed to keep the ego in its place, to remind the monks of their humility. Venerable Simi observed that Westerners seemed to have quite a time adopting the practice of bowing. Some never do. It didn't bother me. It was just something they did, and I didn't mind respecting their ways while I was their guest.

Each day I explored the well-groomed grounds, throughout which were scattered the monks' spartan kutis. Frequently I'd catch the flash of saffron robes gliding swiftly through the shadowy bush. I loved passing the reedy pond where the chirping of crickets, frogs, birds and other bush sounds greeted me. A sign on a nearby tree urged..."In this place of peace, friend, tread reverently, and peace shall be your friend." Whoever placed that sign surely spoke my thoughts. "Reverence"--that was the feeling.

Sid and I spent our first afternoon with the English monk, Rob, whose monastery name was Venerable Darama. We walked and talked for hours. When the bells rang for seven o'clock meditation, Venerable Darama said it was okay to miss the meditation. He'd explain to the abbot.

As we conversed with Venerable Darama, I was fascinated to realize that becoming a monk didn't mean that one had found the answers to life. We were listening to a man, quite human, who had his doubts and who was seeking purpose and looking for assurances --just like the rest of us.

I wondered, how could anyone commit to monkhood without surrendering to the all-knowing wisdom of that God which he follows? I remembered reading how St Francis's disciple Bombarone had said, "The mind is God's lawyer and as such is a great separator from God." I felt that Venerable Darama was a man striving for unity with God, but that his active brain, like a lawyer's, kept him so preoccupied that he couldn't simply listen to, surrender to, and trust that God.

Venerable Darama and certain other monks struck me as men who lacked self-confidence and self-esteem, and I wondered if the monastery experience perpetuated that. So much of the monastic life was designed to diminish the ego and promote humility. Did that help or hinder those people who arrived there lacking a strong sense of self?

We also discovered that most of the men at the monastery had terrific issues regarding women. I wondered if that is another reason why men become monks...or women become nuns.

I spent the morning of the second day being mostly mindful of my empty stomach. Finally at half past ten, we sat down on the floor of the eating room, ready for our meal. First though, we had a long wait while the monks who had stopped their construction work elaborately re-wrapped their robes.

Just as I thought we'd get down to the business at hand, a young Thai family arrived. The mother, father, and little girl all carried bags and boxes of food. They removed shoes and bowed deeply. There was a smiling exchange of Thai words with the abbot and the little family disappeared into the kitchen to place their traditional offerings to the monks on the large counter. They had brought three delectable sauces, curries, meat dishes, and iced fruit in coconut milk. Since all food was donated, the monks ate whatever came, including meat, with gratitude.

I appreciated the tradition that spawned those simple offerings. The Thai family seemed happy to bring their contributions. By supporting the monks who represented their religion to them, it became their way of practicing and participating in that faith.

Finally the monks took their big black bowls from the woven

95

orange bags that they always carry over their shoulders, and at last we filed into the kitchen to help ourselves to the meal. Back in the eating room, the monks placed their bowls on the little stands they carry in their bags. Still we didn't eat. We chanted. A blessing was said. Moments of silence were observed and we waited while the abbot peeled fruit into his bowl. Then he picked up his dessert bowl of ice cubes and fruit in coconut milk and poured it in with the hot food in his begging bowl.

I understood the reason for this action. It demonstrated the acceptance of all gifts with no preference for one over the other. Also, by ceasing to prefer and evaluate such things as food, we become more aware of how we do the same with people, events and circumstances. A person who is totally unevaluating can perceive all aspects of life with equilibrium. Ultimately, the Buddhist is to accept all conditions in peace, and live with harmony and balance.

As I observed the monks, I found it difficult to reconcile some of the differences in their teaching and in the structure of the disciplines. Monks practiced spartan eating habits, yet had conveniently designated chocolate to be a non-food. While I'd been starving, the monks were munching chocolates! Although their teachings espoused the principle of Oneness, the structure seemed based on separation--separating monks from lay people; women from men; nuns from monks; seniors from juniors, and so on.

As I sat on my hillside, I finally realized why I was there. It was to put to rest my urges toward the monastic life. I *liked* solitude. My creativity bloomed, my spirit reinfused when I had quiet, silent time. But my style was not that of a nun or a monk. I *liked* the world--the laughter and tears, the singing and spontaneity, solving problems and helping others. I'd thought the monastery structures would enhance my inward turning. Instead, they disrupted it. Just then I spied a mother roo and a joey grazing on the hillside, and I knew that my own style was that of one who found balance in solitude or with nature rather than with systems, structures and dogmas.

The next morning as Sid and I climbed into our car to leave the monastery and head east, I blessed my freedom. How many of the monks, I wondered, would have loved to drive off to travel, fun, companionship, work, purpose...at their choosing? I'd seen in other circumstances, how people could become trapped once they were completely immersed in the comforts and commonalty of an organization. They get stuck and don't know how to leave even though they might want to.

And I understood the value of coming to the monastery. I'd thought I needed a place where I could sit and walk and contemplate God. Now I knew that, for the time being anyway, the answer was otherwise.   Smiling at Sid I said, "Let's go. I don't want to *contemplate* God. I want to *express* Him."

My Nun's Kuti, Bodhinyana Monastery.

GAWLER AND THE EMISSARIES

OUR 2500 KILOMETER drive to the east was the kind of trip where you hunker down to chew off the miles. We watched our progress in agonizingly slow inches forward on the map and by ticking off roadhouses bearing names like Widgiemooltha, Murrambidgee, Cocklebiddee, Madura, Caiguna. These places were usually nothing more than a cluster of stations and motel buildings seemingly dropped like a pile of litter in the midst of the hard, baking grey-green land.

The Nullarbor Plain separating the east from the west, is aptly named. Nullarbor derives from the Latin, meaning "no trees." The two-lane transcontinental highway ran just far enough inland so that it was impossible to glimpse the spectacular coastline bordering the plain on the south. Once, however, we detoured down one of the few dirt roads that led to a view point. Standing well back from the edge because of the gusty wind, we surveyed the towering, white limestone cliffs which dropped straight and sheer into the brilliant blue Southern Ocean.

It was the school holidays and, despite the heat, Australians were on the move. Mothers and fathers, children and dogs struggled stiffly out of air-conditioned cars, stood in wilted clusters by petrol pumps or under shady overhangs, and waited in lines at toilets or food counters. Having carried out this distraction, they dissolved back into their vehicles for another stint on the uninterrupted desert road.

Some of the roadhouses were surprisingly sleek. At Eucla, for example, we found an attractive, modern complex. We ate in a shiny, tastefully decorated air-conditioned restaurant and treated ourselves to a room in the new motel. Borders of flowers and succulents lined the path to a big, cool swimming pool--which was a real tile and stucco affair, not a fiberglass tank as in so many places. The place presented quite a change from traveling in the old days.

Finally our great push across the Nullarbor was behind us. A friendly sun shone as Sid and I cruised along the rural road to Gawler, South Australia. We sailed atop rolling hills of golden, grain-filled fields and sheep dotted paddocks, and dipped between the hilly green vineyards of the Clare Valley. After passing through several delightful little Germanic towns, we entered Gawler around noon.

On the southern fringes of Gawler, we located the Emissary community of Hillier Park. When we arrived, we found that, unfortunately, the directors whom we'd met in California were away in Singapore. However, others at the center quickly invited us to stay and made us feel most welcome. The Emissaries are an organization which has communities throughout the world. They are people who have found value in living together in accordance with certain principles. Sid and I knew very little about these people or their principles, but wanted to learn more. We'd met some Emissaries in California and had liked and respected them, and had looked forward to meeting their Australian counterparts.

The members of the community lived on the back portion of a large, pretty property, and they owned and ran the Hillier Caravan Park in the front. As soon as we entered the caravan park office, Sid and I felt the uplift, the friendliness and warmth exuded by those whom we met. Luckily, a hire van was found for us. This was not easy because the community was hosting a big, holistic health conference and there was little extra space available.

Marc and the lively Cecile showed us around the grounds before and after dinner. Purchased by the organization only ten years ago, the caravan park was beautiful--one of the nicest caravan establishments I'd seen: clean, open, quiet, pretty and shady, with two pools. Notices for the caravan park's social club, tai chi lessons, travel outings and other activities were posted on a bulletin board.

There was that same quality about this enterprise that we'd noticed at the Emissaries' California facility. Nothing was slapdash. Everything was carefully carried out with thought not just to the utilitarian needs, but also for the aesthetic needs and enjoyment of the inhabitants. Simple yet unique ideas promoted well-being. A bucket and mop in the bathroom invited users to participate in maintaining its sparkling cleanliness. Signs were worded in positive terms, like the one at the pool: "If you respect and care for others at this pool, they will do the same for you." The place of course, was a reflection of the quality of its people.

At dinner we all served ourselves from attractively presented platters on a buffet table and then ate at individual tables in the dining room. As soon as Sid and I came into the room, someone immediately asked us to join them. We had no chance to feel awkward or uncomfortable. People talked freely, and genuinely cared to know us better.

In the kitchen, cleaning up with some of the group, conversations flowed. Adults and children alike were outgoing and reflected confidence, vigor, curiosity and an inner well-being. I was drawn to these happy, strong self-sufficient people and felt that I would like to count them as friends--the kind that I would want to write to and return to over the years.

I didn't know then, that indeed, we would return to Gawler several times in the coming months. I *would* write and share and grow with friends at that community.

Gawler lies 35 km north of Adelaide and is the gateway to the wine country of the famous Barossa Valley. In my earlier travels I'd not taken the time to explore this area. Now, I found Gawler picturesque and appealing like an old peasant grandmother. The central town took its shape from the winding course of the Gawler River, a bone dry, steep gulch snaking under a canopy of magnificent gum trees. Like a worn patchwork scarf, narrow streets uncurled from the town center stamped with patterns of little, old fashioned houses and old time gardens.

Some older parts of Australia are still dotted with deteriorating dowagers of crumbling pink or yellow stone structures. When Sid and I drove south from Port Augusta, we had seen them standing alone in open fields or shadowed under old groves of trees. The streets of Gawler stair stepped with such edifices. Most were postage stamp size with sloping tin roofs and verandas. Next to them, the smooth-sided brick rectangles of contemporary buildings looked incongruous. Sidewalks and gardens were lined with ragged stucco or stone walls giving the place a frontier flavor similar to that of the old mining towns in the Sierra Nevada foothills or the adobe villages of New Mexico.

Gawler's grandmotherly main street, dark, faded, and weathered, bustled with activity in a noncontemporary sort of way. Old men stood chatting in twos and threes. Women carrying wicker baskets ambled in and out of shops, stopping here and there to talk animatedly with acquaintances. Frock shops displayed dresses of that country style that flaunts fancy sheens and lace, but fails in its attempt to look classy. The usual displays of butcher and fruit shops, take-outs and news agencies intermixed with those of appliance stores, stock agents, one book shop and a variety store--all looking slightly dingy and mishmashed. I found it a refreshing change from the so slickly organized presentations of contemporary stores, which seem to spring from the mold of some universal marketing director.

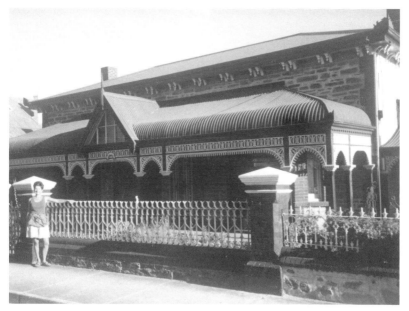

Typical old-style Gawler house.

On our second day in Gawler, Sid and I joined a cheery mob of Gawlerites celebrating Australia Day (January 21) with a free outdoor breakfast. The Apex club, which also spearheaded the nationwide Christmas event, Carols by Candlelight, organized this annual breakfast to which everyone was invited. Local merchants contributed the food.

When we arrived, the shady riverside park already buzzed with families and seniors and youngsters sitting on lawns or at folding tables, drinking tea, coffee, and, yes, beer. Behind long tables the local service club folks in aprons and digger hats served up endless heaps of sausages, eggs, hamburgers, bacon, ham, beverages and a special treat of damper, a kind of bread that bushmen bake in the coals of a fire.

Although Sid and I were intrigued with the old town of Gawler and with the glowing Emissaries, we were now close to the towns where many of the friends lived whom I had come to see. Eager to push on, we left Gawler and the Emissaries after a three day's visit, vowing to return to explore both further.

Main Street, Gawler.

MELBOURNE

OUR ROUTE SOUTH from Gawler became a chain link of reunions from one night to the next. The first reunion took place right in Gawler with my dear friend, Joy. She had come from Melbourne to help her father while his wife was in the hospital with cancer.

When I lived in Keith in 1968, Joy Jaensch (pronounced "Yench"), became my closest friend. Despite the fact that she was several years older than myself and the mother of five children, including a baby, we shared fun, crazy and heartful times together. We'd sit up for hours at night talking after Ed, her husband, and the children were in bed. Sometimes we spent days and weeks creating and planning surprise gifts, jokes, parties or special feasts. In the summer, we'd deposit the kids at the town pool, go to the bakery and load up on buns and bread, and then sit in the car watching the kids while we stuffed ourselves--all the while laughing, scheming, joking or philosophizing together.

No matter what Joy put her mind to, she brought to it an irrepressible enthusiasm and drive. It was thanks to her letters and encouragement that my family eventually trekked to Australia...and once there, it was thanks to her forthright, accepting personality that my parents and I became closer than we'd ever been before. Although the Jaensches sometimes lived close to the edge financially, Joy was determined to visit me in the United States. She got a job working in a roadhouse, saved and scraped up money in any form she could, and *came*.

Now we reunited after ten years. Although Joy's face was creased with wrinkles and her hair was grey, the resolute jaw and intense, sparkling eyes had not changed. Laughing and crying at the same time, we fell into each other's arms and embarked on a new cycle of relating. The vivacity, glow, wit, and deep heart were as bright as ever, but a new dimension was now added to our relationship--maturity. We both had been tempered by the difficult passages of recent years and we both had come to the awareness that our direction, strength and peace all lay within.

Joy had to be back in Melbourne by the end of the week. It was decided that the three of us would drive there together, pausing for brief visits with our friends along the way. Sid and I would return to South Australia later for more in-depth reunions. Thus began our marathon drive south, stopping each night at a different old friend's place, most of whom Joy also knew. It was a happy, chatter-filled time of reconnection--both in the car with Joy, and at each place we stopped.

At the end of the week we arrived in Carrum, the Melbourne suburb where the Jaensches lived. The entire family--including five children and seven adults--lived communally in a large home. It was strange to suddenly meet these people who in my memory had always been children--but who were now adults with wives and husbands and their own offspring.

Once again I was enfolded into the big hearted warmth and generosity of this bright, talented family. The time sped by in day-long and night-long sharings--mostly with laughter, sometimes with tears--punctuated with wisecracks and bottles of beer and an incredible welcome and acceptance that greatly touched us both. In one of his letters home Sid wrote, "Barbara is sort of a legend with the Jaensches and I could tell from the very start that they were glad that she finally returned after twenty years. It seems that they have saved anything and everything that would remind them of her--pictures, clothing, letters, artwork, etcetera. And as they recalled the memories of her year of living with them, I could easily see that they considered her a very special member of their family."

Although it was often overcast, Melbourne's February weather was summery with temperatures that required nothing more than shorts and shirts during the day and no covering at night. Now and then there was a little rain. Once Sid and I took an hour's walk along the Patterson River near the Jaensch's house and got caught in a brief summer shower. It soaked us through, but it was fun, and we were air dried by the time we arrived home.

Sometimes we could feel a hint of fall in the air. Leaves were turning and a few were falling, reminding us that winter would be upon us in three months. We didn't mind, though, because our "plan" was by that time to be enjoying the tropical warmth of Queensland. This was a happy delusion since we couldn't then guess that soon our lives would become so bound up in a special place in South Australia that we would prefer to remain in the cold rather than leave for the warmth of the north.

The Jaensch home was about an hour's train ride (The round trip cost $3.60.) from downtown Melbourne. Sid and I made several day trips into the city and we enjoyed walking throughout the sophisticated metropolis getting a feel of its pulse. There were beautiful parks with lakes, rivers, fountains and wildlife. The Victoria Market, at the north end of the city center was a gigantic complex of Victorian style outdoor stalls bulging with everything from produce and sheep skins to thread and fur coats. Throughout the city, flags and plaques and even the patterns of flower beds, proclaimed Melbourne's (unsuccessful) campaign to host the Olympic games in 1996.

A lot of new construction was going on. Sometimes I'd go off on my own and come back to find that Sid had spent hours supervising backhoe jobs, demolitions and the work on several high-rise buildings. We were intrigued by the variety of small shops operated by people of many different nationalities and by the large shopping complexes sporting the highest of fashions and prices to match.

But the people were the biggest attraction. On almost every block in the downtown center we encountered entertainers--including mimes, guitarists, jugglers, hawkers, flutists and vocalists. We both loved to pause--sometimes for long spells--to watch the entertainers and the people watching the entertainers. At the monstrous Victorian stone edifice of the central railway station, we stood to the sides and watched fascinated as crowds of people hurried hither and thither.

Our visa situation was favorably handled at the Department of Ethnic affairs, where, after a long wait in line, we were quickly granted a six month extension to our visas. We also learned, to our delight, that we had multiple entry visas and, therefore, could come in and out of the country as often as we might choose in the course of the next seven years.

Joy and I had one day out on our own. Her choice was to go op shop* hopping. She picked new territory for her--the Richmond area. The old suburb reminded me of Geary Street in San Francisco where all the ethnic shops are. Trams and autos and heavy trucks roared, screeched and clattered in the wide crowded street. Rows of little shops ranged under old fashioned roofs and stone fronts. Aromas from take-out foods of every ethnic extraction assailed us. Fruit and flower shops were colorfully intermingled with Italian groceries, Greek delis and Lebanese bakeries. We joined the busy bevy of bustling walkers, Joy's trained eye, like a falcon's, readily discerning the op shops.

In each shop we'd dig through piles of clothes and other used goods, questing for those perfect items that would be treasures to us and no one else. I looked for jogging shorts and Aussie T shirts, while Joy searched for clothes and little gifts for her huge family.

On another day, I came to Melbourne alone and walked all over. In the late afternoon my steps took me to the Domain, into the embracing peace of green groomed lawns, palms of every variety, ferns, lakes, gums and gazebos--all so near yet so remote from the busy heart of Melbourne. I traversed the gardens from my tram stop on Domain Road all the way to Alexandra Road bordering the Yarra River. There, in the still high six o'clock sun, I joined other outdoor celebrants who walked, bicycled or jogged along the grassy river bank. Our attention was river-directed where bevies of crews-- mostly made up of men--sculled in long boats. Often the coaches kept pace with them, peddling bikes on the shore and shouting directions through fog horns.

Benches and barbecues were attractively spaced under the trees lining a sweeping drive and walkway above the river. It was a soothing and pretty place to come and be quiet after the bustle of downtown and before entering the homeward bound commuter fray.

Coming to quiet and to writing had been difficult. How could I express the collage of images, faces, and feelings pressing upon me?--The friends we'd reunited with in South Australia--Joy, my bright, enthusiastic friend, so giving and eager--Margie (the eldest daughter), serving me and Sid as she served everyone, seemingly without consideration of running out or wanting anything in return.

How big-hearted the Jaensch family was--insisting on giving us the biggest room and the best bed in the house, and showering us with demonstrations of generosity: Margie loaning me her guitar to take on our travels, xeroxing pages of music and manuscripts for me, hauling out her suitcase full of pressed flower material and teaching me to make the same beautiful cards she does; Ed coming home from his week working with the railways in Ballarat and spending all day making pasties or cooking stews or frying meats; the boys drawing us maps and bringing home special videos and considerately smoking outside instead of in the house; and the food, the glorious food! Everyday we ate a tantalizing feast created from Margie's or Robert's culinary efforts.

Chinese dinner at the Jaensches. Left to right: Peter, Joy, Vicki, Barbara, Sid, Robert.

As much as Sid and I were eager to return to South Australia and pick up the new threads of old friendships, we also wanted to take advantage of our proximity to some of Victoria's most famous areas. Numerous people urged us to visit Wilson's Promontory National Park a couple of hours' drive south of Melbourne, and for years I'd heard about and wanted to see the penguins on Phillip Island. It was decided that we would travel to "the Prom" and take a much needed break from the intensity of the last three weeks. We planned to rent two caravans and, in a few days, Joy and Margie, and Margie's little daughter Janna, would join us there.

Our final meal with the Jaensches was a heartful, joyful, energetic demonstration of the talent and the giving of that family. Candles, crystal and lacquer chopsticks gleamed on the big kitchen table. Robert and Margie worked all day without pause, (well, Robert did nearly finish a flagon of sherry with a little help from Sid) preparing every possible variety of Chinese food. Rob and Margie brought out each course and we oohed and ahhed and gobbled it down while they kept cooking, readying the next course. The meal spread over four hours--and, I fear, our girths. Two of our group fell by the wayside--Peter left after the sweet and sour and Vicki, Rob's wife, after the lemon and ginger chicken. But Sid and Joy and I manfully indulged right through the desert of lychee, jackroot and mango in coconut milk, before staggering at midnight to our bedrooms as firmly stuffed as a trio of Chinese spring rolls.

The next morning, after rising late and blitzing through our packing, we left the Jaensches amidst a flurry of hugs and goodbyes and headed south toward "The Prom."

THE PROM

RED PAINTED CUPBOARD doors and drawers hung open. A bare light bulb gleamed weakly from the white ceiling. The only sound, besides that of the whistling wind, was the periodic clutchety-clunking of the antique refrigerator.

Sid and I thrived on contrasts and certainly life was throwing them at us. From a chattering household of six to twelve people crammed into closets and overflowing into the living room, we came to sitting alone in a sprawling, four bedroom farm house savoring the echoing silence. From the previous night's marathon meal, we came to heating a cup of instant soup. From the constant interaction and requirements of response, we came to an uninterrupted personal flow of walking and sitting, my playing the guitar and Sid daydreaming in a chair.

We were lucky to get the old farmhouse--situated just four km north of the entrance to Wilson's Promontory. We had phoned the Prom from Melbourne and were told that what little accommodation they had was booked solid for the next two months. We travelled south anyway, prepared to stay in a cabin or caravan in one of the several little hamlets that nestled 20 km back up the road.

When we arrived in Yanaki, however, Sid saw a sign on the store (i.e. the town), advertising a farmhouse for rent. We were directed to the dairy farm where the owners lived and learned that "by chance" the people who had booked the house for the week had had to cancel. We snapped it up.

The farm house was perfect for our needs. We had the run of the rambling rooms and could at last spread out and sort our gear. There was plenty of space to accommodate Joy, Janna and Margie and still maintain our privacy. In the nearby paddock, our personal sheep, waddling under a mound of grimy wool, waited to run up to us for a handout whenever we stepped outside the door. Across the road, fresh milk from the owner's dairy awaited us. All for $27 per night-- the same price as a cramped caravan.

In the mornings I wrote at my desk which looked out on a view that stretched as far as the horizon. On sunny days, bands of golden light would streak across the yellow fields which looked much like those of the California coast lands. Swales of bushy green gum trees and low growing shrubs bordered the farm's roads and fences. Wooly grey and white clouds patterned the patches of blue sky. Occasional flurries of birds swept skyward or alighted on the fence posts or on the lawn. In the grassy pasture beyond the front fence, volunteer agapanthus' frilly white heads jutted on slender green necks.

In the afternoons we'd drive to the Prom to hike. The Prom was a magical place. Its 130 km sequestered at the bottom of the Australian continent contained some of the most spectacular and fascinatingly varied scenery we'd ever seen. We hiked on high brooding mountains of granite boulders and along sea-facing sandstone cliffs etched with dense heathery shrubs. We walked through heathlands, marshes and forests made up of high twisted trees. We ambled beside the clear, tea-colored water of slow winding rivers. We body surfed in turquoise waters beside unblemished white beaches. And we moved silently through dense, primeval forests where the rich, peaty earth was spattered by splashes of sun streaking between the lacy, yellow-green foliage of tall tree ferns.

The park was renowned for the tameness of its birds and animals. At the campgrounds and visitor facilities located at Tidal River, we stood with other delighted tourists as waves of bright scarlet and purple lorikeets swept around us, accepting offered tidbits or simply alighting on heads, fingers and shoulders as if these were their own private perches.

Everywhere we walked, we kept an eye out for koalas, which were supposedly roosting in the high trees. People would pass us on trails and say, "When you get to such and such a place, look to the left and you'll see the koalas." Or we'd see arrows and the word KOALAS scratched in the dirt of the trail. But we never saw them. Sid and I did encounter, on one of our long hikes, a pair of wallabies dressed in exquisite, chocolatey-colored coats of fur.

We always planned our return drive home to coincide with dusk when the dark figures of wallabies and kangaroos congregated to feed in the darkening meadows. We were particularly on the lookout for wombats, the cuddly furry creatures who looked like a cross between a tail-less beaver and a pig. The wombats fed on the roadside brush and, when caught in the bright car lights, they'd scuttle away doing an accelerated version of their usual "waddle and crump, waddle and crump". Sadly, these gentle creatures were diminishing in number because of their vulnerability to fast moving cars. Everywhere along the road, signs cautioned motorists to drive slowly for the sake of the wombats.

One day, while Janna, Margie and Joy hiked around the Tidal River area, Sid and I trekked to the top of Mt. Oberon, the Prom's highest peak. The path wound upward through granite boulders which soared amidst pockets of tree ferns and the dense bush of tall, long-limbed gums. The last several meters took us straight up the craggy spine of a rocky outcrop where steps had been chiselled into the stone and where handrails aided us.

When we had clambered high enough to peep over the final rim of rocks, I caught my breath. It was like looking into a magic, silver world. Grey-green foliage draped below us in folds of hillsides converging into the fantastic patterns of undulating shoreline. Around the out-jutting land and distant islands the ocean shimmered like a sun-struck mirror. Sunshot sections of sky streamed silver rays into the glistening surface of the water. We watched as perfectly defined squalls scudded dark curtains of rain across the sky and sea.

Along with several other hikers, we sat on the massive grey boulders and surveyed the most southerly segment of the Australian mainland. Far below, the long wide swath of Norman Bay Beach, broken by frilly white lines of breakers, gleamed beside the silvery sea. The expanse of ocean glinted like burnished metal reflecting the shining sun pockets in the grey streaked sky. Landward to the north, the grey-green ridges of the Prom pouted dully under the gauzy skirts of dancing mists.

After a while the wind and cold got to us, and we clambered back down the boulders just in time to hike back to the car in a fine steady rain. As we walked, Sid and I joked about the delights of summering in Australia--the land of endless sun and drought.

Our hikes usually began or ended in the area of Tidal River, where I always felt as if I were gliding into the folds of a fairytale forest. Long thin, sinewy tree trunks massed like thousands of grey, hemp ropes dangling between the ground and the hidden sky. The trunks grew so close to one another that, had we attempted to penetrate the forest, we would have been lost within a few feet of the path. Twenty feet overhead the branches of these stringy trees merged in a thin, busy roof of green foliage. Seen from overhead no one would ever guess that an eight food wide path meandered below.

The "Fairytale Trail" at Wilson's Prom.

Although it was summer and every available campsite and cabin was booked, we never felt as if we were in a crowded place. By American standards, this national park was delightfully unpopulated. On most of our wanderings we frequently had the trail to ourselves. I admired how the park's quality had been maintained. With its popularity and its proximity to Melbourne, I'm sure it would be very tempting for the park service to double the Prom's numbers of available accommodations. Thankfully, though, the Prom remains low-key--a park where visitors can become part of a unique Australian landscape without having that experience--or the park-- destroyed by the pressures and discourtesies of crowds.

At the end of the week, we all packed up our gear. Margie, Joy and Janna returned to Melbourne, and we departed our lovely little farmhouse and said farewell to the Prom. We planned to return someday, though, because the Prom was the kind of place that one could come to again and again and it was always different, fresh, and inviting.

Dipping in a sea pool at Wilson's Prom.

THE PENGUIN PARADE

ANYONE DRIVING INTO the sleepy-looking town of Cowes would never guess that the tiny resort is the focus of an international tourist industry. Located on Phillip Island, 145 km south of Melbourne, Cowes hosts the constant stream of pilgrims who come to see the fairy penguins returning each night from a day at sea.

A pretty town, Cowes offered several caravan parks, motels and campsites. Although it was late February and the height of the summer season was over, most of the caravan parks remained full. We managed to find accommodation at the local Backpacker Hostel where for $23 a night we were assigned a roomy caravan with an annex. The manager was a special sort of businessman. He provided free transportation for guests travelling to or from Melbourne, and he readily loaned his van to hostelers who wanted to make a day loop over to Wilson's Promontory. Delicious family-style meals were also available. The price of $5 included glasses of wine which, not infrequently, were served up at the bar by the manager's eight-year-old son.

On our second day in Cowes, Sid and I finally saw koalas. We stopped at the sanctuary near town and ambled under the fragrant gums. The way to find a koala was to look for clusters of people pointing fingers and cameras up at a tree. Approaching one such group, we tilted back our heads and saw high above us a furry burr curled in the V of two limbs. I was surprised at how high up he was. No wonder my past attempts to see koalas had fallen short. I'd looked too low. This rotund fellow was cradled in the next to highest notch of limbs--where they appeared very pliant and willowy. Snoozing comfortably in his little lounge, he seemed oblivious to the gaggle of gaping tourists below him.

A man pointed out another koala in the gums just outside the sanctuary. Our eager group hurried over to peer up at him. He dozed curled on his haunches like a huge, furry Poo Bah high in the roof of the tree, one front paw curled around a limb, the other in his lap. Nonchalantly, he lay in the forked branch, swaying two feet left and then two feet right as the wind fluttered the ceiling of leaves in which he roosted. Infrequently he shifted the position of an arm or a leg, perhaps stretched one arm overhead, or languorously scratched under his chin with a hind foot.

I couldn't understand how the people could loudly chatter, joke and smoke in the presence of these wild creatures. My inclination was to whisper, to proceed in hushed silence, as I would in any place of reverence. I felt awash with the privilege of being allowed to intrude into the animals' domain where it seemed that they at least deserved privacy and peace from prying man.

That night at the Penguin Parade we once again were privileged intruders into the world of animals. Breathlessly we watched as a tiny band of the smallest penguins in the world rose out of the sea. Their bodies flashed black and white as they fluttered in the water for a final few meters before stepping on to the sand. Like tiny wind-up toys they waddled, the silvery white gleam of their chests silhouetted against the white frilled tiers of black waves. They tarried, standing in small groups of five or so--perhaps blinking in the bright stadium lights that flooded the beach. Every night at dusk these dainty creatures returned from a day's feeding at sea to step into a blaze of floodlights before a hillside hubbubing with an international audience.

Sid and I had arrived two hours early for the nine o'clock "show." From the visitor's center we descended a wide, wooden walkway. It cut between the slopes of tussocky sand dunes and ended at a gigantic block of double-winged cement bleachers which faced the darkening beach. A young American helped us decide where to sit. He told us not to sit on the bottom tier of bleachers because the tour bus groups would come in later and sit on the sand in front of us. It was best, he said, to secure a spot on the sand now.

While Sid held our places, I returned to the visitor's center. Along the way, I saw clusters of people looking out at different mounding areas on the hillside. Joining them, I saw my first view of the penguins. They stood outside their burrows or squatted just inside the burrows' entries. Were they aware of or oblivious to the gaping humans? Were they, like seasoned performers, blase about their audience? This question would follow me throughout the evening and I still wonder.

After surveying the fascinating exhibits in the modern visitor's center, I returned to the beach and the bleachers. The wooden ramp between the sand dunes could have been a corridor in a cosmopolitan air terminal. The diverse sounds of many languages floated throughout the crowd. Mostly, though, I found myself being carried along in a current of Japanese faces chattering Japanese words. Back at the beach, the bleachers simmered with an international tourist stew. And the diminutive reasons for this commotion appeared on time at 8:45.

The penguins didn't hurry homeward after emerging from the sea. Instead, they huddled in groups by the water--perhaps discussing the quality of the night's crowd?   Should they play to it or not? Evidently making a decision, a little band darted forward, stopped, and then scurried back into the water. They splashed rapidly around in a tight circle before once again slowly attempting the shore-- where they huddled like children unsure of what to do next. Perhaps it was stage fright? Ten minutes passed and then, as one, the group began waddling toward us. They were amazingly tiny--as small as kittens--and their progress scuttling over the sand seemed, at once, comical and courageous.

What luck that we sat where we did. We could nearly touch the scudding groups of penguins that fluttered directly toward us before abruptly turning toward the sand dunes and the routes to their burrows. They were only four feet away from me, scooting like darting leaves, waving themselves across the sand with their wing- like flippers. Once past us, they disappeared up the dark hillside of tussocky grasses, and we turned our attention seaward once more, waiting and watching for the next group to appear.

After nearly an hour, we, and most of the crowd, left the bleachers and dawdled upward along the ramps, stopping to study the softly illuminated sand dunes. Baby penguins who had been waiting all dày for the return of their mothers now bawled out a noisy cacophony of sounds. It was like hearing a chorus of crickets, bird chirps, crow caws and human baby cries all at once. The penguin offspring, who were nearly the same size as their parents, danced in circles around their mothers and snapped up the offered food.

It was moulting season and we saw some raggedy, big, fat, double-sized birds. Normally the penguins were clean-lined, with sleek, blue-black and white feathers, but now grey, fluffy patches of feathers stuck out or fell from their bodies. Before moulting, the penguins ate a lot and swelled to twice their normal size. They then lived off the fat while they fasted for 14 to 17 days. Fewer birds, we were told, went to sea during the moult, because without their feathers, they were no longer waterproof and would drown.

As we continued walking up the ramps, we saw little lumps of birds sitting or standing alone or in pairs. Some still straggled homeward, some looked lost, waddling back and forth as if trying different routes. A few squatted like statues in the shadows. Others darted energetically along the trails. Many a bird sat solitary and immobile beneath the beams of the ramp's lights. Would they have hurried straight home if we weren't there, I wondered? Did they sit still waiting for the humans to leave? Were *they* taking *us* in? Were our two species united in some auspicious form of mutual entertainment?

As I had done at the koala sanctuary that morning, I wished that the people would be quiet. They quipped and joked, talked loudly and pointed. Children wailed. Camera flashing was prohibited, but done anyway. Children ran loudly about slapping tennis shoes on wood and pavement. The smell of smoke, perfume, shaving lotion and fast food assaulted me and floated toward the burrows.

I wanted to protect the diminutive creatures from the thwacking of running feet and the witty wisecracks of the peering people. The penguins seemed almost dazed. I couldn't help but wonder how different their behavior might be if there were no chatter and lights. Surely our presence intruded.

500,000 visitors a year trek to Phillip Island. Dozens of tour busses ply the route between Melbourne and the Penguin Parade visitor's center. Most tourists don't stay the night, preferring to round-trip it back to Melbourne after a day's touring. I wondered where did the penguins fit in this astounding commercial enterprise? Was this the best entertainment the *animal* kingdom has ever seen?-- thousands of people herded into fenced walkways and bleachers, then grouping in all forms of attire and shapes to peer over fences into the night? Did the penguins sit on the hillside dunes doing nothing because they were absorbed in the human sideshow?

Or were they and their artless pilgrimage victims of the great human selfishness carried out in the name of education? It was with a mixture of elation and sadness that we left the penguins...elation for having glimpsed their gallant daily life, sadness for the intrusion that mankind brings to it.

*   *   *

Three days later we headed north--to Melbourne and on to South Australia. Ahead lay welcome and participation such as we'd not yet experienced. We were about to plunge into a way of life with which we would both fall in love...so much so that we would forego migrating to Queensland with its sunny winter weather.

"WONGARY"

SEVERAL KILOMETERS SOUTH of Naracoorte, in the South East of South Australia, Sid and I turned our car into the gracious stone-walled grounds of "Wongary." "Wongary" was the palatial old home and vast sheep property run by Diana, my AFS sister, and her second husband, Robert. On our southbound trip to Melbourne we'd spent one night there and glimpsed the rich, varied and hard-working life which Diana and Robert led. Ever since that visit, Sid and I had eagerly anticipated returning to "Wongary" to become part of that way of life.

We quickly found ourselves fitting into the "Wongary" existence, which offered us a delightful place of settlement and involvement. The day of our arrival Rob and Diana had just signed the papers acquiring a third farm. On the following day, we watched as Rob, Diana and helpers scurried back and forth to the barns busily preparing 400 stud ewes for a massive artificial insemination program. Sid spent that entire day assisting Rob and had the best time he'd had in weeks.

Rob and Diana were people who thoroughly immersed themselves in their work *and* play. An extremely conscientious farmer, Rob took great care to maintain and improve his stock and land. This involved an incredible amount of know-how and hard work. Much of it was physical, but a lot was sheer mental: the calculations of sheep per acre if the sheep were big, vs if they were small, vs if there was feed, vs if there wasn't, vs if the sheep had long, thick, or short wool, vs if the market was up or down, vs how much chemical to use, vs if it rained or not, and on and on. We were impressed with Rob's management skills and the magnitude of the decisions and work which he directed daily.

Sid loved the farm work and being a friend to Rob in many ways. After a sunrise to sundown chock-a-block day, Sid crashed, having reveled in learning the art of building fences; learning to rewire farm houses Aussie style; making the rounds of the 34 paddocks (every three days) to feed the sheep and to check or clean the water troughs; herding sheep from the back of a motorbike; hefting ewes into position for artificial insemination; attending tractor pull contests; harvesting alfalfa; yarning with the blokes; digging ditches for electric lines or fence posts; sludging around the bottom of rain tanks removing muck; repairing broken down harvesters; helping Robert and Diana figure out their new Agri-Master computer program....He was in hog heaven!

Rob, a tall, slightly balding man who wore glasses, was at once a sharp, hard working farmer and a Teddy bear. His gentleness slipped out when he referred to his teenage daughters and when he was yarning with the older, neighboring farmers. The previous year Diana had undergone a mastectomy and she tenderly told us how wonderfully helpful, caring and understanding he had been.

Rob's playfulness showed up in playing pranks with his children and with the AFS students who occasionally came to live at "Wongary". Sometimes I'd hear thuds on our cottage door and look outside to find Robert throwing apples at it. Other pranks ran to making Australian country music tapes for friends but inserting a risque, gauche and sleazy Kevin Bloody Wilson song. Eyes twinkling and grinning broadly, Rob was constantly making sly, low-key remarks that caught us off guard. Both he and Diana kept us rolling with laughter with their quick-witted repartee.

To see Diana was to see a sparkling woman intensely involved in conversation, erupting with jokes and laughter, hopping up and down or falling sideways in her chair or on to the floor in order to emphasize her point. In twenty years, her appearance had hardly changed. She was as slim and well proportioned as a teenager, and except for the tiny lines creasing her eyes, she could have passed for her daughter. She was the kind of strikingly attractive woman who looks different in every photograph, yet is always stunning and photogenic.

As the director of the Naracoorte Art Gallery, Diana thrived on presiding over art functions, sitting smartly-dressed on art boards, and contributing her organizational talents in many ways. At the same time she kept the household end of "Wongary's" business running smoothly. She produced delicious farm meals for the jackeroo*, Rob, Sid, and the frequent drop-ins of ten or more. She ran the computer programs for the farm, and dropped everything to herd sheep, man the field burning, or whatever other of the many farm jobs needed attention.

Diana's creativity channeled into numerous activities--like designing an elegantly comfortable home and garden, sewing stunning outfits and organizing events--from elegant parties to bush breakfasts. When her children were younger, she'd coax them into escapades such as painting black zebra stripes on white ponies, or painting the apples on the trees red. At the same time, she was a thoughtful, articulate woman who enjoyed the art of playing devil's advocate in conversations. She was also an astute businesswoman who managed the rental of four houses as well as being a partner and co-director of "Wongary". A keen observer with a fascination for local color and history, she produced a steady flow of short stories about different aspects of motherhood, relationships and rural life.

I found it quite remarkable when I thought how the seed of this time had been sown 27 years ago. Diana's vivacity, humor, and self confidence had inspired me ever since she first danced across the barriers of my carefully polite family. We had shared and grown as

Diana, Robert, Barbara and Sid in front of "our" cottage.

121

teenagers, then as young women when I lived in Australia, and now we were doing so again as mature (?) women. As we prepared meals or shopped or walked together, the hours clicked by crammed with quick smatterings of sharings, racing off on tangents, heartfelt exchanges, and catching up on the growth and events of people and years.

I felt close to Diana in ways I hadn't before. As she read my writing and commented, she opened me to the writing possibilities within me. I learned from her example about how to present my work to newspapers and magazines. One article was immediately published thanks to her advice, and we collaborated on other pieces. As teenagers, Diana had opened me to spontaneity, play, boys, femininity. Now she was helping me give birth to my writing career. How interesting the cycles were and how I had wound up at "Wongary" at this particular time.

One reason things worked so well was that Sid and I were rarely underfoot. We had our own little, rose-covered, yellow stone cottage a few steps from the big main house. On the outside walls a flagstone stairway wound to an upper room of sloping roofs which we turned into my writing "garret." From the upstairs window, I could look out through a webby screen of maroon-leaved branches toward the big, black fish pond, ex-swimming pool, across the way. As I sat writing, the tree's branches bobbed with rotund, little birds nodding and chirping sociably to me. From the dirt drive below wafted a noisy cacophony of farm sounds--the clattering of tractors and harvesters, the high-pitched whine of motorbikes, the roar of heavy trucks and the bleating of mobs of sheep being driven beneath my window.

Downstairs were our twin beds with bright patchwork quilts and the "kitchen"--a hot plate. The toilet and water were a few steps across the lawn in an outdoor laundry building. We showered and cooked in the main house, crossing a large garden fragrant with ripening autumn produce. Apple and pear trees hung heavy-branched, littering the lush lawn beneath them with red and gold fruit. Every morning I "figged-out," gorging myself on ripe figs from the prolific tree next to the goat and pony paddock. In four weeks I ate more figs than I had eaten in the course of 45 years!

During the day the four of us were generally scattered in different directions. At night we came together to enjoy sharing the evening meal. Despite the men's tiredness, we often lingered at the table talking about all kinds of things. Sid and I were gratified to see that we seemed to fit in to Diana and Rob's lives, rather than being an intrusion.

Although both Diana and Rob were very playful, exuberant people, the stress of running the farm was tremendous, especially for Rob. With the passing of each year, he found it harder to accomplish everything he wanted to do. He was a perfectionist who preferred to do jobs himself rather than delegate them to the workmen. Making and carrying out plans was frustrating. Interruptions were rife. There were bush fires to fight. Stock agents spontaneously dropped in. Sheep showed signs of worms and so the entire mob had to be mustered and drenched*. Foxes killed lambs, so nighttime spotlighting forays had to be organized. The harvester broke down in the middle of the job (which had to be done NOW before the rain came)...No wonder Rob sometimes wound up with headaches. I gave him his first-ever massages, sprinkling the sessions with some relaxation suggestions. He responded well and kept saying how much more relaxed he felt--until the next heavy pressure came along.

Diana, too, began employing some ideas about relaxing and letting go, and not trying to control everything. She started going for long walks, often carrying Sid's hand-held tape recorder so that she could note whatever creative thoughts came. One day Rob told us that he had walked in on Diana meditating. Diana showed me a letter to her daughter in England in which she had said, "As we adopt many of Sid and Barbara's philosophies and learn some of their methods of relaxation, both Robert and I have increased our personal happiness." She continued for two pages describing our "philosophy."

As she read the manuscript of my book, Diana offered me some excellent suggestions. She kept saying, "Hurry up and finish it...I want to read the next chapter...You should get it out to the world." With that kind of encouragement, my motivation level flamed, and I hunkered down in my upstairs garret putting in hours on the book.

Besides relishing the time for writing, I reveled in the countryside.

After writing for most of the day, I'd set out to walk for a couple of hours. As I ambled along the hard, clay road between golden paddocks that rolled away to the horizon, I saw a classic farm scene. Woolie lumps of sheep busily browsed, heads down, rumps up. Magnificent multi-colored and twisted red gums arched over the roads and dotted the fields for miles. Leaving the pastureland, I would follow an old, sandy track leading into a patch of wild scrub that was like my private bit of heaven.

My days were also full visiting with two local women who were going through confusions and fears because they had recently been diagnosed with multiple sclerosis. In Perth and Albany and now in Naracoorte, just as had happened in the U.S., there was always some link that brought me into contact with people who were going through difficulties or transitions. A phone call would come, someone would drop in, a friend of a friend would be mentioned-- and I'd find myself meeting wonderful, new people and being able to give to them from the storehouse of my own experience with illness and change. Although the two women read my manuscript, what

Tree dotted paddocks at "Wongary."

was best was the time we spent talking and sharing with each other. It was a rewarding connection for all of us.

I was interested to learn that there were *lots* of MS folks in that rural South East area. I don't know what the statistics were compared to the city, but I strongly guess that MS in Australia is primarily a women's affliction and that it reflects the male/female experience in that country. Many Australian males present a facade of toughness, chauvinism and righteousness. Their women seemingly support this by impassively going about their business of raising babies, making homes and accepting social interactions where the men congregate on one side of the room and the women on the other. I agree with Dr. Brugh Joy* that MS is about resentment, and I think there are a *lot* of Australian females who are full of resentment.

Sid and I enjoyed meeting the Naracoorte locals and Diana and Rob's friends. There were some delightful social activities: tennis afternoons with the ladies, a gourmet wine and pub dinner with more ladies, the Naracoorte Art Gallery openings with Diana, and an incredible concert with Ted Egan, one of Australia's foremost balladeers.

One outing we attended was the AFS potluck in Naracoorte. It was amazing to discover the international community sequestered in this sparsely populated district. The crowded residence where the dinner was held was sprinkled with students from Finland, Germany, Malaysia, the U.S. and Canada, as well as Australian students who were about to leave for, or who were returning from, overseas. Diana was the oldest AFS returnee present--it was 27 years since she had lived with my family!

One very gracious dinner we enjoyed was at a friend's farm near Kalangadoo, an hour's drive away . On arriving, we all trooped, in our evening finery, out into the potato paddocks to view the crop, then inspected the bulls, the shearing sheds and the harvester. Inside we sat down to an elegant crystal and silver, six course meal complimented by several bottles of superb local Coonawarra wine.

We also strolled in awe down a long gallery of Hans Heysen paintings. Hans Heysen is perhaps Australia's most renowned artist, and Tim, our host, was his grandson. The paintings were *so* Australian, and revealed Hans' deep love affair with the trees. He

125

captured early rural scenes of farms and drovers and tree-tunnelled roads, all of them including diverse studies of the magnificent red gums that characterize this South Australian area. The paintings, Diana said, were so priceless as to be uninsurable.

That Tim's house still exists is a miracle. While the rest of his farm burned around it, the house escaped the devastating 1983 Ash Wednesday fires that destroyed millions of stock, houses and farms in three states.

The days at "Wongary" were slipping into weeks, and then into months. I was getting much writing done, helping out with farm activities, making new friends, and savoring my private times in nature. Sid felt purposeful and that he was giving, and he was excited about all the farm things that he was learning. We felt warmly welcomed, deeply involved, and except for brief excursions away, we found no reason to leave.

THE SCRUB TREES' GREETING

No one comes to greet the scrub
   to sit in stealing shadows hearing
   flitting, tweeting birds and
   magpies' raucous morning bleating

In the lean, untempered trees shimmering
   gray-green, white bark gleaming,
   misnamed Mess Mates without accounting
   for the hidden lives they're screening,

But those who penetrate on sandy track
   into the circle of its meeting
   softly savor the scrub trees' greeting.

               "Wongary" March, 1990

NEW LAMBS FOR "WONGARY"

I SPENT A fascinating day watching Rob's men as they carried out the artificial insemination process on the stud ewes at "Wongary". Because the cost of stud rams has soared to thousands of dollars, Artificial Insemination (A-I) has become cost effective and Australia leads the world in perfecting this high-tech form of breeding.

The amount of work involved in redirecting nature is tremendous. Two weeks prior to the event, the 400 ewes had been carefully prepared with hormonal implantations so that they would have a timely and extended cycle. Two days before the big day, each ewe had its implant removed and received an injection of pregnant mare's serum to encourage multiple ovulations.

Ultimately man had to rely on Mother Nature, and the day before the A-I, a castrated male, stimulated with testosterone injections, was placed in the paddock with the target females. Strapped to him was a pack of blue powder. Following his urges, he jumped on every ewe that was in heat, leaving a blue mark on the behind of those who inspired his desire. The unmarked ewes were then removed to nurse their disappointment in another pen.

On the morning of the A-I, the vet and his assistant arrived bearing containers of freeze-dried semen from a selected ram. An assembly line was set up. First the ewe was caught from a nearby pen. She was then hoisted by three men onto a metal cradle where her legs were locked into stirrups. There she was turned upside down, hind legs up in the air, belly eye level with the seated vet. After a quick shave and a wash of her underbelly she was wheeled over to the vet.

Making two rapid razor cuts on either side of her underbelly, the vet inserted an 18 inch long fiberoptic tube on one side. Through this tube he pumped gas to expand organs away from the fallopian tubes. Looking through the tube, which was like a microscope, I could clearly see the ewe's pink pulsating organs. On the sheep's left side, the vet inserted a pipette (a long, clear, straw-like tube) of semen with a needle and syringe. He looked through the fiberoptic tube while wiggling the pipette, then at the right moment, he punctured the fallopian tube, saying, "Now," to his assistant who compressed the syringe sending the dollop of semen into the correct spot.

At this point, the ewe, looking more perturbed at her undignified position than in pain, was wheeled away. Her incision was sprayed with purple disinfectant and she was released--apparently none the worse for wear. There was virtually no bleeding, and the entire operation took a minute and a half per sheep. As I watched the casual way these men lifted, pinioned, cut into, and handled the sexuality of these animals, all the time carrying on conversations, I thought how similar it was to the way some gynecologists handle their women patients--as if the female herself was unrelated to the task at hand.

Two weeks after the insemination, a ram with a blue powder marking pack would again be introduced into the paddock with the ewes. The resulting marks would enable Robert to determine which ewes were pregnant. They would then be separated from the other sheep and maintained in their own exclusive flock, so that when

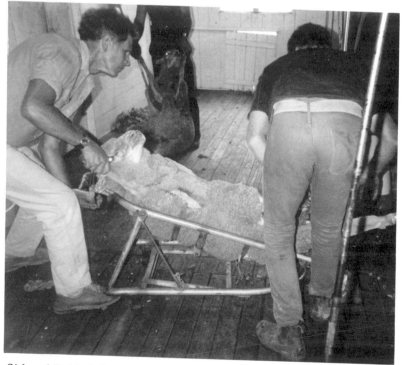

Sid and Rob's helpers prepare an A-I ewe.

lambing time came there could be no confusion as to which lambs were A-I progeny.

This particular process of A-I was more reliable than the old-fashioned methods. The vet, who came from a town two hours away in Victoria, had perfected the operation. His entire practice was made up of such work, and he had traveled all over Australia, as well as to South America, demonstrating his skills. His encouraging words to Rob were, "You can expect 60 percent conception, but taking into account the number of twins born, there should actually be 100 percent live births." We all eagerly anticipated the end of June when the results of this day's handiwork would start appearing in Rob's roadside paddock.

THE WETHER TRIAL

THE SHEARING SHED at Bunn Springs Farm, a couple hour's drive from Naracoorte, was a colorful, noisy hive of activity. Farmers in work-stained Akubra* hats animatedly swapped news and drank beer and coke, while surreptitiously eyeing a table displaying shiny silver trophies. An electric wool press clattered, compressing piles of wool into big hessian bales. These were stenciled with black letters and numbers before being stacked at the end of the shed ready for collection. Outside, dogs barked, men weighed sheep, and dust spiraled as gaggles of sheep skittered from one pen to another.

This was the scene of the annual Wether Trial results. Breeders from all over Australia had picked eight wethers (gelded male sheep) and sent them to the control farm near Keith, South Australia. Producers could compare the performance of different teams and lineages as they were maintained under identical conditions for three years. Our friend, Rob's, sheep had participated throughout the project and placed well: Fifth over all.

The Trials' results were tallied on numerous large charts nailed up on the walls of the shearing shed. Sid and I needed interpreters to explain the meaning of the maze of hieroglyphics indicating microns (the fineness of the wool), gross fleece weight, cleaned fleece weight, the percentage of the yield, price per kilogram and price per fleece, the price from each year, the grand total after three years, etc.

The goal of the Trials was to provide information regarding wool profitability. Like everything else in farming, this was a gamble because market demands change. In recent years fine stranded wool had been popular, but it might not be in the future.

We met many farm characters and their wives, and heard a fine speech by the Australian Wool Corporation (AWC) representative. He discussed the world wool market and the problem of overproduction. This was ironic, since the point of the Wether Trial was to research, measure, and encourage the increased production of the most profitable wool.

Regarding women working in the shearing sheds, the representative said, "I take my hat off to them...You never see them standing around waiting for the next job. They're always busy... Our shearing level has come up since women came into the sheds..." Diana explained to me that few women were actually shearers, but in the last decade many had become shed-hands or helpers.

The representative discussed the horrendous problem of "contamination" in the wool. We learned that all sorts of objects ended up in the bales: tools, wire, twine, paint, bottles, and even dead sheep.

There was also the problem of staining wool by marking sheep with certain spray paints. He held up a can, pointing out, "It says right here: Use only around the head." But not all farmers read what's on the can.

The problem of arsenic and other residues was brought up--how buyers would no longer accept wool containing more than a certain percentage of pesticide. (Arsenic is used in sheep dips. Besides penetrating the wool, if carelessly disposed of, it can seep into the ground and infest the feed.) Farmers were having to change their life-time habits and some didn't like it. But the AWC encouraged them, knowing that it would make for a better and more acceptable product in the long run.

I was impressed at the enlightened attitude of this man from the AWC. He was talking about what vitally interested the farmers--production and marketing--AND LINKING IT with the importance of observing certain ecological and environmental standards. He could have been a Green Peace representative.

After his speech, there was a barbecue and presentation ceremony and more yarning. I had a chance to gather up some unique souvenirs to send to friends--a bundle of red notebooks presented by the Elders stockagent company. Pocket-sized with a pencil snugly fitting into the spine, they were perfect for farmers to whip out and record sheep numbers or do calculations. Besides which, it includes such handy hints as liveweight and imperial/metric conversions, breeding tables, a display for checking earmarks, how to measure tanks or dams, first aid for snake, spider, and lizard bites, artificial respiration instructions, etc.

(A 70 year old American friend responded to her gift saying, "The little red book you sent is invaluable! I can now startle and amaze dinner guests with the exact date a sow will drop after a January 12th service.")

The trial results seemed quite erratic. One year Robert's sheep placed fifth, the next they placed seventh, and this year they were in 19th place. But still in the grand tally, they came out fifth overall. Rob could be pleased with this result, for it gave him a measurement of his sheep's economic productivity and the breeding quality of his rams. It was also a wonderful promotional tool to trot out when he was advertising or negotiating sales.

Having learned all this, we set off for home under the sparkling sky. Unfortunately, we left before the final results were announced, so Robert was unaware until later of his accomplishment. He missed the chance to make a speech, but his trophy, an inscribed silver cake server, arrived via another farmer later that afternoon.

Men weighing sheep at the whether trial.

WOOLY QUESTIONS

WOULD YOU ASSUME that the point of farming is to produce as efficiently as possible, the highest quantity and quality of product? Would you further assume that since Australian farmers have been doing just that, they must be laughing all the way to the bank? In fact, farmers are devastated, and their main trips to the bank have been to restructure loans.

Throughout our stay at "Wongary," our friend Robert, along with the entire Australian wool industry, had to confront some heavy duty questions. The wool market was drastically affected by the 1989 political and economic changes in eastern Europe and China. At the same time, Australian farmers had so improved their efficiency that there became a huge over-production of wool.

The Australian Wool Corporation (AWC) had established a floor price for wool. If no one offered to buy above that price, then the AWC would buy the wool to keep in reserve awaiting a rise in buyer interest. By March of 1990, they had run out of funds paid in by member farmers to maintain the reserves, and were forced to borrow in order to buy surplus wool.

Even the Arabian market for sheep meat had dropped. During the last 20 years, Australian farmers had delighted in being able to send aging sheep to the Saudi market. The Arabs wanted male sheep they could slaughter in accordance with their religious beliefs. A big market developed and air-conditioned boats capable of carrying 110,000 live sheep at a time plied the route from Australia to Arabia. In the fall of 1989, though, the Arabs, striking while the wool market was sinking, turned back Australian sheep ships.

As wool prices continued to drop, farmers, quite naturally, shifted to selling sheep for meat instead of wool, and they glutted that market. A sheep sold to the Saudis for $27 twelve months before, now brought $7 on the local markets.

This was where the difficult decisions came in. Should a farmer continue to invest in or should he dump a product that might become worthless? Winter was approaching. There was no feed in the paddocks, and no rain in the sky. Sheep must be fed from grain stores. Paddocks needed to be planted with feed crops and to be fertilized and chemicalized (in Robert's case, at a cost of $3,000 a month). Sheep still needed to be drenched (given costly medication) for worms, crutched (shearing away the wool from around the tail to prevent fly strike which can kill the sheep). Wool kept growing and sheep must be shorn--regardless of whether or not the wool would be sold.

Breeders like Robert had invested huge sums in careful breeding programs. Robert had just had 400 ewes artificially inseminated from prime blood lines, at a cost of over $10,000. What would he do with the prize lambs when they arrived in July?

Sid and I were participating in the farm life at "Wongary" at a unique time--as Robert confronted decisions that could make or break him. He ran a high tech, efficient, educated operation and was geared to breed and produce large quantities of high quality wool. He *could* diversify and grow other market crops besides the alfalfa seed which he already produced. He *could* shift to cattle, as he'd done in other down times along with other farmers, over-loading *that* market. But his expertise, love and investment was with Merinos. Without a wool market, however, and with the dwindling meat market, he had no certainty of income. He went to meetings and employed experts and tried to plan.

Diana said that they never played the lotto or the TAB* or gambled in any way. I could understand this, since farmers must already be the biggest gamblers in the world, gambling with their livelihood every day. First there's the weather gamble. Robert and other South East farmers were experiencing the driest, warmest autumn in 50 years. Normally, by May Robert would have been finished planting oats for the next year's feed crop. It didn't rain, though, and his $18,000 seeding machine sat idle. This was especially frustrating since instead of selling the current year's oat crop, Robert was pouring it into the 12,000 sheep that he had to pay laborers to help maintain--while he waited for the meat and wool markets to revive.

At "Wongary" all domestic water came from rain caught in ingenious gutters from the roofs. There were nine rain water tanks totalling a capacity of 17,000 gallons. By the end of autumn these contained less than 1000 gallons for seven residents--the lowest the reserves had ever dropped. Fortunately at a pinch, there was a large supply of underground water to fall back on. Windmills provided bore water in the paddocks and in the garden and toilets, but it wasn't very palatable.

Incidentally, there was also water above ground. Those foreigners who expect Australia to be bone dry would be surprised to gaze across the grassy fields around Naracoorte and see large lagoons, ponds and swamps. These were typically studded with sepulchral, grey trunks of dead gums and dotted with prolific flocks of black swans, ducks and other water fowl.

For farmers, how much the wool market would revive was a big gamble. During the 1960s, Australia was hit heavily by the growth of the synthetics industry. At that time many farmers were weeded out. Now farmers were talking once again of massive losses. Experts likened the situation to the carriage making trade when automobiles appeared. A busy industry was set up to produce carriages efficiently, but once cars supplanted carriages that industry simply disappeared. Even the usual means of reviving industries--war--no longer works in these days of synthetic soldiers.

The whole issue of sheep farming has become a very wooly question. Sid and I were fascinated and impressed by the chains of cause and effect that Robert and other farmers must consider. There was no question of the Hoopers surviving--in one form or another. As Diana said, "We've been through down turns four times now. Everyone thought the industry was done for in the seventies. We tightened our belts then and we can do it now. It always cycles back."

COMMUNICATION GOES TO THE DOGS

ANY ARMY GENERAL, corporate officer, or parent will tell you that the success of an order depends on one's ability to communicate. That is what a dozen farmers learned at a three day sheepdog training workshop held at "Wongary" in April. Few of the participants realized beforehand, however, that Neil McDonald, from nearby Keith, would be teaching them the same principles that skilled psychologists use.

Neil, a fit, thirtyish fellow, was a forthright speaker who easily maintained class involvement while simultaneously monitoring dogs and owners practicing routines in the background. Questions were easily and thoroughly answered. Whenever Neil used dogs from his own stud to demonstrate how something should be done, everyone stood riveted, admiring the skill, responsiveness, and grace of his intelligent animals.

Neil frequently taught by drawing colorful analogies. For example, he likened a new dog to a new delivery employee who must be given time to become orientated before he can understand how to choose parcels or how to convey them to their correct destination.

"Most farmers," said Neil, "are looking for an 'All Rounder'--a dog who can do everything." Finding an All Rounder is as difficult as expecting a cricket player to be able to play all positions perfectly. Rather, farmers should have three dogs: one who is good at paddock work, one at yard work, and one who does a bit of both.

Some dogs are naturally inclined toward paddock work, silently stalking sheep and keeping them moving forward in an invisible "bubble." These dogs are independent and quite capable of working without instructions from owners. Other dogs incline toward yard work. They are "Power Pumps" who bark, charge, and leap on sheep's backs moving them as directed in pens and chutes. "I've seen good dogs shot because farmers didn't understand how to use their dogs," said Neil.

What if you have the right dog in the right job? How do you elicit the best performance from him? According to Neil, this is where communication is vital. "Dogs only do what we allow them to do." Generally dogs are born with the ability to work well and to please, but uneducated owners kill that. For example, if an owner gives unclear commands, the dog tries to guess and gets punished if he's wrong. "How motivated is he going to be to try again?"

As Neil talked, I became aware of his overall theme; i.e. the same principles that apply to people, apply equally to dogs. Many of us remember school situations where we were unsure of an answer, tried, and were scolded for getting it wrong. How motivated were we to try again? Dogs and people "go timid." "Timid," said Neil, "is a word we use for *our* inability to train."

"It is the *owner's* behavior," stressed Neil, "that determines the quality of a dog's performance." What behaviors should an owner practice? One is to have reasonable expectations. "Don't expect the dog to do what it hasn't yet learned." Another is to communicate clearly. "Be specific. Which paddock. Which sheep. Which gate." Neil demonstrated how owners can apply these behaviors at many levels.

Neil and his amazing dogs demonstrate their skills.

The first level is to get the dog attentive to *you*, instead of scattering his attention all over the paddock. "Program the pup never to go between you and the mob. He should stay by you, not tearing over fences into the sheep." By stamping his feet, speaking sharply, and jerking a rope to the dog's neck, Neil quickly had a young dog sitting attentively. By making it uncomfortable for the dog to look elsewhere, the dog decided he *wanted* to look at Neil.

Then Neil tugged steadily on the rope. The dog's resistance could be seen in the straining of his body. When the dog moved forward a bit, Neil released the pressure. "Pressure. Response. Reward," explained Neil. The dog *chose* to sit facing Neil, the rope hanging loose.

Neil likened the dog to a student and himself to a blackboard. The dog was required to keep his attention on the "blackboard" as Neil stepped in circles around him. It only took one sharp toe shove in the hindquarters before the dog pivoted whenever Neil even slightly moved that foot toward him.

How few sheepdogs have mastered this level of responsiveness was comically demonstrated on the first day of the workshop. Neil had the participants take their dogs into a large paddock and turn them loose. A well trained dog will walk directly behind his owner awaiting commands. This paddock became a riot of barking, chasing, leaping dogs--and sheepish looking owners.

"I reckon that dogs have a comic gallery for men," said Neil. "We stamp our feet and scream and they turn their noses up at us laughing up their sleeves. It's not the dogs that are the idiots, it's us."

Like children, dogs will burn with desire to work and to please if reinforced in the things they do best. "The goal," said Neil, "is to let him be a winner." Many of Neil's comments emphasized ways of employing positive reinforcement:

Look at it from the pup's point of view.

The dog should work *with* me, not *for* me.

Make him feel important.

Make him *choose* to work, then he won't see work as an imposition.

This last comment Neil also applied to sheep. He teaches that as you train your dog to work appropriately, so the *dog* will train the sheep. Ultimately, even the sheep will *choose* to be worked.

At the "Cut-out" barbecue, participants excitedly discussed the improvements in their dogs. Neil said, "I reckon I'm proud of my students. It's not easy to exchange old habits for new ones, and I admire you for being willing to invest as much time in your dogs as you do in your rams or utes."

Perhaps the ultimate acknowledgement of the workshop's success was shared by one repeat participant who commented, "I've been applying these principles to my wife and kids for months."

"Has it made any difference?"

"Too right!"

IT'S A WAY OF LIFE

IN THE DISTANCE a tiny tractor slowly trundles across a paddock, bringing to mind John Williamson's song, *It's a Way of Life*. For I'm seeing a way of life that is under threat, that is rapidly dissolving in this modern world. On that tractor sits a man who is self-initiating and self-determining, who waits on no work scheme of tea breaks or bonuses. He decides his own daily schedule without assurances of wage minimums and rebates, and to him the concepts of striking, time padding and clock watching are completely alien. The man on the tractor represents independence, self-sufficiency, confidence, commitment, drive, courage. His is a way of life that sets an example for the rest of us, and its dissolution is increasingly accelerated as big economics and big politics play their games.

The Australian wool situation was becoming more critical by the day. It is a complicated story, but the main point is that the floor price for wool was being dropped. It needed to be, since it was too high. But the government stewed about the decision for over a month. Can you imagine listing your house for $80,000, but telling buyers, "Maybe I'll be dropping the price next month."? Naturally the market, which was already poor, went to hell in a hand basket.

On top of having their wool income slashed, the autumn's drought swelled Rob and Diana's expenses. The unprecedented dry weather was clobbering South Australian farmers. Normally, by mid-June, the paddocks should have been lush carpets of rich green grass. Since they weren't, farmers had to supplement feed. Rob spent five hours a day just feeding. Every time I drove past a paddock with sheep lined up eating distributed hay or grain, I knew that some farmer was paying through the teeth to keep them fed.

And it was more than "just" feeding. It was quite complicated. Originally Rob fed a combination of oats for fibre and triticale* for high energy. But the sheep needed more protein, so he shifted to pure triticale. Even though he carefully and slowly introduced the change, many sheep reacted, evidently not having built up enough intestinal bacteria necessary for breaking it down. Foundering like horses, they lay down and would have died unless Rob came along

141

and heaved them on their feet. Appetites and food intake were affected, weakening the ewes. Lambs were aborted or birthing was difficult, particularly with twins.

Despite Rob's effort to properly feed the newly purchased ewes on his new property, Quince Hill, many of them lacked the strength to push out their lambs. He had to spend hours a day assisting the ewes to give birth. Every time he saved a ewe and a lamb, though, it was another mouth to feed. By then, the market price for lambs such as these (once they were bigger) was what Rob called an "acceptable" $30. The year before, ram lambs had fetched $45, but now Australian farmers had lost that Saudi Arabian market.

I wondered, *What will happen to Rob's precious Artificially Inseminated lambs, when they're born in July?* He took special precautions with the inseminated ewes, feeding them heavily, organizing spot-lighting to eradicate foxes before the lambs began arriving, checking the ewes frequently. But always there was the doubt--are they a good investment? In a normal market he could count on the lambs being snapped up by breeders, and fetching as much as $400 each. Instead, Rob now faced the prospect of having to feed, medicate, crutch, shear, etc., until such time as buyers surfaced.

Before the drought, Rob had contracted with a local supplier, at a set price, for 20 tons of lupines. But the dealer backed out, forcing Rob to buy later-harvested, inferior quality lupines at a higher price. The lupines came from a drier area where lots of wild radish seeds got into it, so Rob's worker, David, spent whole days with a borrowed giant sifting machine separating the lupines from the radish seeds. The seeds would have created havoc in the paddocks where Rob grows his "certified pure" alfalfa and clover commercial seed crops.

When at the end of autumn, sparse rains finally came, they set off a plague of red-legged spider mites on the long awaited green clover that sprouted in the paddocks. The mites sucked up all the nutrients so the paddocks had to be sprayed. In the past Rob would have hired a plane to do this, but he was now saving money, so despite the chemical dangers, he and David went out every day spraying.

Once a month Rob tested for worms. These parasites attach themselves to the sheeps' intestines, sucking blood from the lining.

If symptoms surfaced, Rob had to drench (medicate) the entire mob. If he was lucky, he could wait and do a "strategic drench" in the summer. Since sun and heat kill worm eggs, the paddocks would not then be reproducing worms even as he drenched the sheep.

One day after Rob had driven all the way over to Quince Hill, the feeder system broke down. He had to return home, spend the day fixing the feeder, then make the half hour trip again to do the feeding.

The day after that, while driving his ute, Rob smelled something burning. Just in time, he stopped and discovered that a rag had fallen down between the cab and the bed and ignited. Thinking quickly, he managed to dowse the fire with the water he carried for washing his hands after birthing the ewes. He singed his hands, but saved the ute.

Diana, Rob and Benny, the dog, culling sheep.

Soon after that, Rob came in from another long day and said, "My dog is dead." Just like that. The dog, which was invaluable for his operations, simply died. There were no symptoms whatsoever. All Rob could guess was that it had a heart attack. The dog was only four years old and Rob had just gotten it to a well-trained stage. He had two dogs left. One, Benny the Wonder Dog, was really too old to be working. The other, Mac, was young and untrained and had a disconcerting habit of requiring that Rob lift him into the ute. Hardly propitious for a sheep dog.

Another night, Rob read us a proclamation from the shearers union, stating the conditions they were demanding: $1000 per 100 sheep; free room and board; pressers, (the men who press the bales) wanted $60 per bale. This kind of news nearly brings farmers to tears. Already they and their wives knocked themselves out readying the sheds, sheep, and equipment, and providing meals and accommodation for the shearing contingent. Currently shearers were earning $135 per 100 sheep.

Rob told us that there once had been times when it wasn't a good idea to hire non-union shearers--a farmer risked having his sheds burnt.

One night after tea, as we recounted Rob's increasing turmoils and obstacles, it became so ridiculous that we all finally collapsed laughing. At that point Diana called across the room, "Rob, the next time you read your Bible, look up the Book of Job. It's about a bloke like you."

On the lighter side, Rob regaled us with the romantic escapades of his and Diana's far-flung family. He had two daughters, Annabel and Jane, from his first marriage. From *her* first marriage, Diana had a son, Tim, and a daughter Anna. Nineteen year old Annabel, (who spoke fluent Japanese, looked like Bo Derek and attended two universities at once) was being courted by an Italian jeweler who wanted to fly her home to Brindisi for a month. There ensued many long distance phone calls between Rob and his ex-wife, the Italian family's neighbor, because the family did not speak English ("We'll guard her with our lives. She will never be left unattended."), and Rob and Annabel ("You have to earn your own money. This must be your decision whether or not to miss Uni.").

The upshot was that Annabel brought her suitor and his brother home to "Wongary" for the weekend. Rob asked the suitor, "What are you going to do if Annabel dumps you after she returns?"

The suitor shrugged and said, "No worries".

Diana said of the proposed trip, "I think it's a great opportunity," and set about helping Annabel prepare for her adventure.

The other daughters were also beautiful and intelligent. Anna was working and modelling in Europe after safariing through Africa. She was currently being courted by a Grand Prix driver. Jane was flying off to join her English boyfriend in London. Diana and Rob jokingly told their three eligible daughters, "If any of you are considering weddings this year, better think along the lines of a bar-be in the scrub."

Tim, who had no interest in farming, was busily sowing wild oats, yielding a harvest of long distance phone conversations between "Wongary" and Adelaide.

Sid and I felt privileged and moved, being able to participate, however minutely, in "Wongary" life as Diana and Rob confronted an incredible scope of considerations. And we wondered, *Where will it end for them and for other farmers?* In a country where laborers do better on the dole than on a job, where states declare race days as holidays, and where paid holidays disrupted the nation as often as four times a month, how would they and their way of life, almost an anachronism, survive?

In 1989 the Australian *Sixty Minutes* TV program presented a segment in which a farmer and a wharf worker switched jobs. The farmer stood around drinking tea with the wharfies while they waited for cargo, drank in the pubs while they struck for better wages, and waited while they refused to handle cargos that were "too heavy," secure in the knowledge that as a wharfie he had a floor level income no matter what.

Meanwhile, the wharfie rose at the crack of dawn, slogged through an unbroken farm day, sank exhausted into bed at night, and sputtered, "No way would I work like this".

The epilogue informed us that by the time the program aired, despite his efforts, the farmer had lost his farm, unable to keep up with the increased costs and 18 percent interest rates.

Already much of Australia's cattle and wool industry is in corporation hands. Who but big organizations with unlimited capital can meet the demands of modern farming--namely paying the exorbitant costs and interest rates?

Our entire society is the poorer as it loses those who are still willing to initiate, decide and direct their own labors. Family farming, though demanding, spawns strong people who have an identity of self-sufficiency, self-respect and courage. That is why, when I look across a field traversed by a lone man on a tractor, I see something very precious. I see a gallant, grass-stained warrior valiantly demonstrating and preserving a way of life.

Lawnmowers at "Wongary."

HAVOC IN THE PADDOCKS

PRETTY PADDOCKS MASK reality. At "Wongary" we gazed upon green fields dotted with grazing, wooly ewes shadowed by winsome, white, skittering lambs. We'd think, *How pleasant. How perfect nature is.* But behind the lovely field was the lack of grass, or the earth mites, or the hours of sowing or chemical spraying. Behind the picture of the cute sheep were days of worry, frustration, mutilation and death.

Rob educated us to the hard work and heartache that could exist behind those placid mother and lamb farm scenes. The autumn's unprecedented drought drastically effected the birth process at Rob's new property, Quince Hill. Because the new ewes and the new property were both unknowns, adjusting the feed proportions was complicated. Despite his knowledge and efforts, the ewes did not receive enough protein. The result was that many lacked sufficient strength to push the lambs out at birth. Every day Rob spent hours over at Quince Hill pulling out stuck lambs.

Aggravatingly, his caretaking simultaneously saved animals *and* increased their loss. Maiden ewes (first timers) such as those with which Rob stocked Quince Hill, don't naturally look after their lambs. When Rob deposited feed in the paddock, they chased the truck, forgetting about their lambs; or when he drove around seeking troubled ewes, the mob scattered. Either way, lambs lost their mothers and died. But Rob *had* to disrupt the sheep. They needed feed, and without his intervention many simply wouldn't survive birthing. It was a vicious, yet necessary circle.

Sid and I took turns accompanying Rob on those rounds, supporting him as best we could as he carried out a heartbreaking, but fascinating process. Rob would quickly spot a downed ewe, or one who looked wrong--walking heavily, stumbling or standing strangely. When she ran from us, stringy birth fluid or tissue trailed from her rear. Often we could just see the points of tiny feet sticking out. Rob would say to the dog in the back of the truck, "See 'er Benny?" and then, "Get 'er Benny!"

Benny leapt from the truck and within seconds he tackled the right ewe, bringing her down. Rob jumped out of the truck and, inserting his hand inside the ewe, would start pulling the lamb out. It was a messy, miraculous process. Slowly, carefully, pulling and working with both hands and even bracing on the ewe with his feet, Rob extracted tiny, slimy lambs. Some were dead. Some were totally ignored by the mothers when he placed them in front of their noses. But what elation we felt when a mother started licking the birth sack and showing an interest.

Once Rob stood up with a lamb and swung it back and forth. He explained, "Sometimes they get fluid in their nostrils. This flushes it out."

When I asked Rob how old he was when he learned to pull out lambs he answered, "I don't remember a time when I didn't know

Rob helps a ewe to give birth.

how. I learned from watching my father." It's simply a part of farming, and these men like Rob don't enjoy it, but they know what must be done and do it.

Sometimes we were too late. A lamb had been partially out of its mother for too long, and all Rob could do was to remove the dead little thing and help the mother up again. Other times were worse. The lambs had decayed inside the ewes. Rob had to extract the foul smelling mess. It was for those times, in particular, that I came along. It was too ugly and depressing a job to do alone. Rob would give such ewes an injection and often, amazingly, they'd stagger to their feet and lurch weakly away.

There were times when in order to reunite a lamb with its mother we brought it inside the truck, where I gently cuddled the tiny, yet surprisingly strong, little creature. When we approached a group of ewes, Rob grabbed the lamb by the scruff of the neck, dangled it out his window and dropped it to the ground. We roared away, leaving the newborn lamb standing bewildered and alone, we hoping that the mother and baby would stumble into each other before the lamb died. It seemed so harsh, yet it was the only way. If Rob walked up to the ewes, they'd run away. If he handled the lambs too much, the ewes might reject them.

In each paddock Rob established several portable three-sided pens from metal fence sections. Ewes that didn't immediately mother their lambs, or pairs that were especially weak, were left there with some hay overnight. It was an effective way of forcing the mother to care for her lamb.

The most critical ewes, such as the ones who were in shock, were hefted into the back of the trailer or ute and hauled back to the barnyard pens. Typically, we'd trundle in with the trailer and truck bed strewn with corpse-like ewes; shivering, bloody, yellow covered lambs; and perhaps one or two orphan lambs at my feet inside the cab.

Putting them into the pens was another heartbreaking event. The ewes and lambs simply seemed to miss each other. Lambs tried to suckle, but the ewes wouldn't move into correct positions. Or a lamb stood shakily bleating while the mother ignored it from across the pen. Once, as we looked at the dismal scene, Rob turned to me and muttered, "Those lambs will be dead tomorrow."

But amazingly many survived. This was largely because Rob further confined the pairs by erecting metal fence pieces across the corners of the yard pens. When we returned each morning, we would immediately look to see what the night's survival rate was. We were thrilled whenever we saw that most of the penned couples wound up bonding with each other.

Always there was some humor in spite of the circumstances. When Rob used the gallon of lubricant for the tough ewes, we joked about having brought it from his bedroom.

One time he said, "I wonder which ewe I left my watch in."

Or he might finish a job, hold out his mucky hands, and say, "Got any sandwiches?"

To lift the occasion to a more upbeat atmosphere, we played rock music in the ute.

One night after tea, Sid presented Rob with a surprise. Sid read from the package: "Good for things that are ooky, pooey, gooey, icky, sticky and sucky."

Rob immediately knew what it was, "Gloves!"

And in fashion colors too. We joked about using the pink ones on females and the blue ones for males. Unfortunately, they were not elbow length, but at least Rob was now able to protect his hands, which were always covered with cuts and scratches, from infection.

As we bounced across the paddocks with our depressing cargo, I sometimes felt like we were a MASH unit. And, indeed, we did speak of "Going into the battle zone." Orphan lambs wandered separated from mothers. Ewes lay on their sides kicking futilely. Lamb bodies littered the grass. Rob told me, "We always expect about 30 percent loss."

But this year was exceptional. Besides the effects of the drought on the newly purchased ewes, they seemed to genetically lack the inherent hardiness to handle giving birth. Rob said, "I've never had a problem like this with my own sheep."

In fact, just to renew his sanity, one day as we drove back from Quince Hill, he pulled into one of his home paddocks. We drove across it admiring the healthy young lambs contentedly feeding beside their mothers. Rob said, "I haven't had to touch one in this paddock. This is the way it should be."

Even when the process was "as it should be," a symphony of

decisions, complications and responsibilities was constantly being orchestrated behind that placid paddock scene. I knew that never again would I casually don a wool garment, tread on wool carpets, or enjoy a lamb roast, without pausing to consider the people, hard work, and heartache which they represent.

Success! Two healthy twins.

After the drought, at "Wongary."

KEITH REVISITED

ON A COLD July afternoon, Sid and I parked beside the Keith pub, and my memories swirled in a kaleidoscope of names and faces. Here, twenty-two years ago, I'd participated in more than a few rousing cabarets. In its dining room I'd sweated through my first lunch meeting with the Area School teaching staff. I, the raw recruit, had sat awed by their easy familiarity, expertise and confidence, while barely comprehending their trigger-fast sentences and Australian accents. When school started the next day, I discovered that understanding the kids was twice as difficult.

Keith was the hub of my existence during 1968. As an immigrant Yank and untrained teacher, I was something of an oddity to that South Australian country community. My vibrant memories derived mainly from Keith's people--from the involvement with teachers, students, parents, friends, and boarding families. Returning now, in 1990, I was struck by the degree of turnover, not only of those I once knew, but of many others.

Rain squalls pelted, emptying Keith's familiar streets and darkening the utilitarian buildings and the few vehicles in their point-in parking places. The street trees softening the expanse of concrete seemed bigger. With Sid, I walked past the house on Morcom Street where I first boarded with the Groves family. Mr. Groves had been the bank manager. Mrs. Groves had graciously helped me correct homework. Afterwards, she used to put out the billy* by the side gate for collecting the milk. Robert, the young son, kept a pet lamb in the yard. Christine, the teenager, was in my social studies class and we used to swap clothes.

From my back porch bedroom window I'd looked across an empty paddock towards the public pool. Lots of splashes indicated a delay before going swimming. Few splashes meant, *Better hurry over before the kids get there.* Now the gums and shrubs in that paddock were so big that the pool was completely obscured.

In that tiny room, I encountered my first Australian "electric blanket." Unlike the American variety, which is a blanket that drapes snugly over you warming the entire bed, this was merely a square pad that one laid on. I'd turn it to the highest setting and roast three feet of my backside while the rest of my body froze.

Keith lies beside the two-lane Adelaide-Melbourne highway. A Soldiers Memorial park and a long street of mostly vacant older buildings parallel the highway. Gone is the deli where I tasted my first Australian hamburger; it was differently delicious, consisting of a patty, white bread toast, fried egg, beetroot, carrot and shredded lettuce, and cost less than a dollar. Today, just a few steps, and another world of food away, is a shop whose presence truly surprised me. Inside *The Penny Farthing*, we found locals and highway travellers sipping espresso and munching quiche and croissants amidst attractive displays of arts and crafts. Down the street is another newly opened craft shop--also vying for the lucrative trade of highway motorists.

We walked to the "hub" of town, past the stock agents offices, the drapery shop, the three banks. *Wormalds*, the chemist, had moved to the town center from a block away where the town used to peter out. The new shop looked slick, nicely-carpeted, well-stocked. In 1968 I'd taken out health insurance at *Wormalds* old store. It had seemed a good idea when a friend invited me to ride her stallion.

Crossing the street, I dropped some letters in the slot at the Post Office and was suffused with a sense of deja vu. So many links with U.S. ties had fluttered in and out of that building.

At the Keith motel I chatted with the receptionist, Heather Cavanaugh, each of us throwing names like darts, mostly off the mark. But one in ten hit a bull's-eye. "Oh yes, the McNabs. They moved away...Christine Groves married Thumper Neave, they're up in the Northern Territory. Christine was on TV talking about the problems of one of the kids. Kidneys, I think it was."

I used to wonder what sharp, clever, country girls and boys would move on to, and I asked about my old students: "Gerhard Schmied, Alwin Goetz, Wayne Bramstedt, Jenny Allen...?"

"I heard Jenny works for the Education Department in Adelaide...I knew Wayne's mum. She used to cook in the pub. She moved away...."

"What about Mr. and Mrs. X?"

"Mrs. X went off with Mr. Y. Mr. X ran off with Mrs. Z."

"Did you know the Nankivells?"

154

"Arthur retired, moved to Kingston."

The Nankivells had been my second boarding family. They'd built a new brick house out on their farm and I moved in along with them. Margaret, Arthur and the children had welcomed me and my sometimes funny ways: odd hour phone calls from California, Mr. Jagger dropping in for tea, my tiptoeing home in the wee morning hours, hitchhiking to outback places like Birdsville and Coober Pedy during the school holidays, sometimes roaring up to the door in a Mack truck. Increasingly, I spent the middle of the week with Mr. Jagger and the Jaensch family at "Windsong". Ed Jaensch managed that sheep property and his wife, Joy, became my friend. Finally I simply moved in with the Jaensches.

The Jaensches transferred from "Windsong" about the same time that I left Keith, but in the ensuing years I maintained my friendship with them and other Keith friends. Mr. Jagger married Miss Neunkirken, the next teacher who boarded with Nankivell's. They visited me in Oregon. So did Miss Lowe, who now lives in Mt. Gambier.

"Last March," I told Heather, "I accidentally discovered that Mr. McGorm is now with the TAFE* and living in Naracoorte. I'd struck up a conversation in the Naracoorte Art Gallery with a big man. After a couple of exchanges he said, "You used to teach school in Keith!" My jaw dropped. "And your name was Miss Miller!" At this I squealed, so that all the heads in the gallery turned, "Oh! It's Jack McGorm! And Penny!" as I recognized the lady next to him as Miss Saunders--now Mrs. McGorm."

My timing for this Keith return proved wretched, because the school was empty--closed for the July holidays. Nevertheless, we wandered the evacuated grounds. A multi-colored mural now dominates the front building, but the biggest change was on the south side. Outside the primary school rooms, sand patches, bushes, mounds and grass scattered in crazy quilt fashion as if sprouting wherever someone had the urge to sink a shovel. Alongside the cricket field, the source of many a meal donated by kids collecting mushrooms, the trees planted at special ceremonies have exploded into tall, bushy masses.

Along the spacious entry drive, convoys of yellow busses, driven by and carrying teachers as well as children, used to roll up and out each day. (We could identify the houses where teachers boarded--wherever a yellow bus was parked in a paddock.) As an Area School, Keith serves children who travel long distances. It was always a concern that first graders had to catch the bus as early as seven o'clock in the morning, ride an hour over rough roads to school, and then repeat the ordeal after three p.m. It was difficult for teachers to know how to discipline wayward students because we couldn't keep them in after school. We all had to catch the bus.

Often on Fridays, several teachers would board Mr. Jagger's bus armed with casseroles, cakes and sleeping bags in readiness for a weekend at Windsong. When Mr. Jagger's bus, which frequently broke down, did so after a weekend sojourn, a gaggle of gleeful teachers would be stranded. Only now do I appreciate what the poor headmaster had to put up with.

Sid and I crossed the drive to the old school grounds with the original weatherboard buildings. Here was my first classroom where I strove, nervously, to conjure up entertaining activities during the first week of school when no schedule, syllabus, books or equipment had yet arrived. There, too, I perched on the desk trying to look masterful, while the new fashion of the times, (supposedly) stay-up nylons, steadily wrinkled ankle-ward.

At the front of the school we noticed an open door leading into what is now the Community Library, constructed in the school and shared by both school and community. During more name tossing with the librarian, I learned that Mr. Wigney is now the headmaster. In 1968 he was the second-in-command, and although gracious, he couldn't have been too thrilled about having an ignorant, untrained teacher--me--on his hands.

Across from the school we stepped into the famous David's Deli, where everyone bought pasties at lunch time. It looked bigger, with wall-to-wall shelves of colorful candy bars, treats, and something definitely unanticipated 20 years ago--videos!

"We altered our business," said David, "after the school put in its own canteen, wanting to provide the kids with healthy menus. They still don't eat healthy. Our customers changed--more adults--bank clerks, stock agents and such. Most of them don't eat breakfast, so they all have smoko*. We're busy as can be in the mornings."

More names darted about. Particularly that of Geoff Gazzard, the previous headmaster with whom David's mum corresponds. I'd never thought of him as "Geoff," he was always "Mister" Gazzard. Out came the family album. There he was--at the beach! In bathers! Holding his youngest child! That authoritative figure so highly removed from the ordinary world that I'd never considered him having something as down-to-earth as a wife, let alone children!

From David's Deli, we walked along Dugan Street entering the Keith Small Engines Shop. In the warm glow of a wood stove, we chatted with Aubrey and Elspeth Taylor, their dog sprawling at our feet. Outside, hail pelted and thunder clapped, while inside, more names sprinkled the air.

While chatting with various people I would ask, "In your opinion what's the most important thing that has happened to Keith?" No one mentioned the arrival of the water pipeline from the Murray River.

Heather, at the pub, commented, "I reckon Keith's going backwards. We used to have three butchers. Now we have two. Used to have two bakers, now we have one."

We discussed how country towns are changing due to the influx of big Woolies* or Coles* complexes in nearby towns. "Yes," agreed Heather, "Whenever I'm in Naracoorte, I always see Keith people shopping there."

She added, "About $150,000s been spent on the Institute.* They're slowly putting on more plays there and holding art shows. But I like movies. There's no movies here."

Even though the population of 700 has stayed about the same since 1968, there's a large turnover. Bankers move in and out, as do teachers. The stock agents employ ten or twelve men who stay a while before being posted elsewhere. "Cattle," said David, "used to be the main industry. Now Lucern seed is the big cash crop." David described Keith's splendid new slaughter house, saying, "Within seven days, our lamb is on American tables."

Twenty-two years ago Keith had been my Australian launching pad. From there I foraged out on weekends and holidays, and later to the West and beyond. It was the place that gave me work and several long-enduring friendships; in Keith, homes and hearts opened as families invited me for tea or even for the weekend. I experienced my first ball, first fox hunt, first drought. I rode my first-ever school bus, passing emus and kangaroos along the way. I learned teaching on-the-job, resulting in my biggest contribution to Australian education--retiring at the end of the year--forever to maintain admiration and gratitude toward those who have mastered that difficult art.

My feeling on returning to Keith was of a twofold sameness. On the one hand was the large list of names of those who'd moved on. On the other were the entrenched roots of those who had remained. As I learned of the leave-takers from those who stayed, I appreciated how solidly enduring were these stayers, how fortunate they were to share histories, friendships and community in this easy-going, little country town. And on that July day, I felt once again warmly welcomed, as long unspoken names echoed in the cold Keith air.

At David's Deli where I purchased pasties in my teaching days.

THE THREE DAY EVENT

EVERY JUNE, SOUTH Australians don their Driza-bones and Akubra hats, attach themselves to one or more dogs, and head for the Gawler Three Day Event. Driza-bones, the oilskin raincoats made famous in the movie *The Man From Snowy River* have become the height of fashion, and people strolled the Gawler show grounds draped in the long brown coats regardless of the sunny weather. Dogs, too, seemed to be de rigueur, and every variety, small to huge, mongrel to aristocrat, pranced, barked, strained leashes, and sprawled beside owners.

Each day I loaded up my day pack and merged into the colorful swirl of fans, families, competitors, horses and dogs, and became a participant in an institution, in a way of life that captured the imagination. It was another of those magical encounters with people who were demonstrating *involvement*. To invest such energy, time, and hard work, one *had* to posses a high passion and a talent for perseverance, patience and meeting challenges.

The first two days consisted of dressage competition, in which the horses and riders strived to flawlessly execute demanding routines in the show ring. Intent spectators lined the fences surrounding the flower-bedecked ring, some sitting on folding chairs or on portable tripod stools. Others set up barbecues and cloth-covered tables and viewed the events as they dined. Each of the four judges sat inside his individual wooden viewing cottage and flashed his marks on large lit-up screens. Banners and signs around the oval advertised tack and equipment. Overhead, Australian flags fluttered on tall flagpoles.

The big attraction was on the Sunday. Several thousand people gathered to watch the Cross Country competition held on private properties in the hills above Gawler. This was the day that really glorified the horses and proved the quality of their training. Early in the morning they completed a "roads and tracks" course--along the Gawler streets--and a steeple chase at the race track. From there, each horse set off, first along the highway and then up a long dirt road, to the hilltops above Gawler.

159

After trotting a distance along the hill's crest, riders reined into a roped off gathering area. Here they had ten minutes to rest and rejuvenate their horses. It was a scene of color and activity. Grandmoms, siblings and spouses sprang to remove saddles, then busily walked, washed and brushed horses. Vets checked the horses' heartbeats, weight, and limbs. Riders paced, helmets under their arms, flicking whips, chatting with trainers, sipping beverages.

Along with the crowds, Sid and I rambled the course high above Gawler's show grounds and suburbs. Beyond, the flat coastal plain fanned hazily to Adelaide and the sea 40 km away. Breathlessly, we watched as the horses and riders negotiated incredible obstacles. I'd already roamed the entire 6 km course the previous day, my excitement leaping as I'd comprehended the skill and courage which I would see displayed. There were huge, wide jumps, some heading straight down/up/sideways on hills. Now we gasped as those perfectly turned out, precisely performing horses and riders from yesterday's dressage ring thundered across hillsides, leaped pipe lines, brick barriers, monstrous logs, beer wagons and rows of barrels. Many of the riders were frail-looking girls.

We watched, hearts in our mouths, as the horses negotiated the aptly named Snowy River Leap, an obstacle where a horse first had to clear a huge jump and then plunge straight down the sides of a ravine. Immediately afterward he had to jump off a high boarded-up bank into a large pond, plough through the water to the far side, wheel around, vault a fence back into the water, bound up a steep embankment, clear a huge hurdle and race on to the next set of obstacles.

This spot, with its sun-flecked, gum-shaded hillside and grassy banks, was the most popular viewing area. Enthusiastic applause flew up for every competitor. We appreciated and thrilled to the mastery of those who flawlessly executed this run. But the ones who ran into strife impressed us, too. For when horses stumbled, spectacularly catapulting themselves and riders into the water, we saw a powerful demonstration of determination and courage. The crowd's coolest teenagers and the busiest beer drinkers gasped, fascinated and applauding, as drenched riders caught up the reins, remounted and continued.

Spectators freely sauntered about the hilly course, which was only casually cordoned off here and there. Parents with children and baby strollers, old ladies with canes, and beer drinking revelers strolled along the dirt track until someone pointed out a horse thundering toward them. Somehow they always managed to step to the side in time.

Dogs and Driza-bones at the Three Day Event.

Much as I was enchanted by the horses and riders at the Three Day Event, my fondest memory was of the dogs. The PAL SUPER DOG TRIAL delightfully surprised and lifted me right into a realm of merriment, effervescence, and pure joy.

One noon in the show grounds a dozen gold and red clad men and women leaped into the show ring and scurried about setting up gold and red obstacles: hurdles, bars, circles, ladders, slides, and a long canvas windsock attached to a dog house. Owners and dogs paraded around the ring and then gathered at the starting line. The female commentator said, "We don't care what kind of dog it is. We like all varieties, from mongrels to aristocrats." It certainly looked that way.

In turn, each owner dashed with his dog up to the first obstacle, directed the dog over the jump, and then raced to the next hurdle. It was immediately obvious that people and dogs were in this for fun, not precision.

As they negotiated the course, each dog displayed its own personality and style. One neophyte collie needed his owner to dart up and point at the obstacle several times and even to run around the hurdle and beckon to him. A black Lab effortlessly demonstrated how an old hand could do it. Some dogs approached hurdles, hesitated, then trotted or turned to their owners for encouragement before deciding to leap. A kelpie mix completed the last hurdle and made one more spring, right into his trainer's arms, to be carried off. The queen of the group, a sleek, grey, long-legged Weimaraner, elegantly swept through the course, never turning a hair, while a little cylindrical dog, surely succeeded more on enthusiasm than on account of her very short legs.

Perhaps the most independent display issued from a lanky brown dog who romped over the obstacles and, with two hurdles remaining, stopped and squatted for what must have been an endless minute for his embarrassed owner. The crowd twittered and the commentator managed to say, "Well, you know how it is, when you've got to go, you've got to go."

At the doghouse, the dogs darted in, forming a streaking burrow through the attached windsock, except for one little terrier who halted, studied the entry, and gingerly proceeded one paw at a time to lump slowly through the long gold canvas.

At the ladder, the dogs were to pause at the top platform for five seconds before descending. This was to demonstrate that they were under the owner's control at all times. It was also comical, as several dogs demonstrated anything but control--skittering down the other side of the ladder after pausing briefly at the top to quizzically glance at their owners.

My favorite dog was a blond, sheep-doggish moppet. When his turn came, the commentator said, "Look out for this one! We never know which way Shaggin will go--sometimes all directions at once! He's here for fun!"

Shaggin hit the hurdles like a floppy torpedo, legs spread-eagled, head sideways, tearing through the windsock, flying up the ladder, and catapulting down the other side. He had no finesse at all, but he had exuberance to the extreme. Like a flying teddy bear, he pelted through the course, grinning as if sharing a joke, and everyone's heart warmed.

Throughout the exhibition, an unseen woman sparklingly commentated, building up each dog's personality, filling in its background and quirks, and making the dogs come alive for us as individuals. I thought it was the best commentary of its kind I'd ever heard, and I wanted to meet the lady who was responsible for it.

Afterward, I entered the cluster of enthusiastic onlookers converging on dogs and owners. Many, like myself, were pointing at Shaggin and asking, "What kind of dog is that?" A Bouvier de Flanders we learned. Someone introduced me to the commentator, a short, stocky lady, with long blond hair. Meeting her became, for me, the crowning thrill of the entire four days.

For Judy Chapman had created what I consider a dream career-- working with animals and promoting their well-being with her expertise. Her business card read: PETCARE INFORMATION AND ADVISORY SERVICE, and included double sets of fax and phone numbers. My curiosity ran wild and I showered her with questions.

She explained, "I advise people on how to care for pets, psychologically, physically, whatever. I line up pets for commercials and TV programs. I do a fortnightly Personality Pet program on Adelaide TV where famous people bring their pets. I organize that."

People on all sides were awaiting Judy's attention. We ended our conversation although there was so much more I wanted to know about this fascinating woman. Judy graciously agreed, though, to meet again and to let me follow her around for a day.

The Three Day Event was a special experience, and, as is so often the case, not in the way I'd expected it to be. The Australian setting, the horses and competitors, the Cross Country course, were wonderfully thrilling. But the three days offered so much more than what I came for. Unexpectedly there were the dogs. There was Shaggin. And there was Judy Chapman.

COOBER PEDY 1968

IT WAS 1968. The silver Cessna glinted and disappeared into the solid blue sky without a hint of acknowledging our frantic hootings and tootings. The car halted its mad race along the dusty track, and Gladys and I leaped out, waving and yelling at the empty expanse. Our gallant driver handed out our rucksacks and we sank dejectedly onto them--after first extracting the bag of jelly beans in readiness for a serious conference. Surveying the cluster of corrugated buildings lining the red dry dirt of the Port Augusta air strip, I thought, "Here I am at the fringe of the Outback. Am I going to miss it after coming this far?"

After six months in Australia, I was champing to see the Outback. As an untrained teacher in the Keith (South Australia) Area School, I was also eager to escape the intense education through which my teenage students were grinding me. Gladys, the home sciences teacher, and I had planned this May holiday's trip for two months. Short and stocky with a close-mowed shock of straw hair, Gladys was an intrepid Northern Territory girl, the ideal companion for an adventurous but ignorant Yank.

To my suggestion of hitch hiking, Gladys responded, "We'll hitch to Coober Pedy! It's a great opal mining center. Miners come from all over the world to work there. It's miles from anywhere and so hot in the summer that the locals live in caves underground. Coober Pedy is the dinky die Outback. Nobody goes there for pleasure. You'll love it."

"What's the road like? Is there traffic?"

"It's a real Outback road," she assured me. "Mostly dirt track. Only the hardiest of vehicles can traverse it, and they travel in convoys of two or more so there's help if one breaks down."

As we plotted our trip, we received plenty of good old Aussie lampooning in the school staff room.

"What if you get stuck there?" we were asked. "What if you get lost?" "You crazy Yanks." "Nobody goes to Coober Pedy."

The ribbings increased along with the reports of unseasonable weather. A deluge raged across Australia's Center and the teachers made sure that we were apprised of every news story.

"It's the worst weather conditions ever for this time of the year," someone read from the Adelaide paper. "Tourist busses, passenger cars, and semi trailers are bogged in the thick, red, bottomless mud of the track stretching north from Coober Pedy to Alice Springs. Parties of sightseers are stranded at Ayers Rock. Light aircraft are dropping supplies to the washed-out parties but some airstrips have even become too wet for landing."

"Have fun."

Secretly Gladys and I reveled in this added challenge of reaching Coober Pedy under the most adverse circumstances. But we also had an ace in the hole--Eric, an acquaintance who sold Cessna airplanes. To my request for a lift to Coober Pedy, he'd initially responded, "I wouldn't want to send my wife or sister there." He must, however, have decided to make the best of impending disaster, for he confessed that, in fact, he would be flying to Alice Springs and could drop us off at Coober Pedy. "Just get yourselves to the Port Augusta airstrip at ten o'clock Monday morning," he said, "I'll pick you up."

We were ecstatic. Port Augusta, only 200 miles north of Adelaide on the Spencer Gulf, was the last outpost, the jumping off place for all those travelling either north toward Alice Springs or westward across the continent's miles of bleakness to Western Australia. With paved road and ample traffic all the way, we had no worries about arriving there on time.

We'd easily achieved our first night's destination of Port Wakefield, about 100 miles north of Adelaide, arriving so early that we accepted our driver's invitation to join him on a visit to the York Peninsula. While he attended to business, Little Glad, as the teachers sometimes called her, and I struck off along the deserted road that ran straight for miles past isolated farms. We hopped and skipped along in the chill autumn air, and we were surprised when a large bronze vehicle passed us, screeched to a halt, doubled back and revealed Jill Manual, the Keith School arts teacher.

We stared at each other in mutual disbelief. Jill exclaimed, "What are you doing here? I thought you were heading to Coober Pedy! You're going in the wrong direction!"

After gay greetings and explanations, as well as some dubious remarks and quizzical looks from Jill's parents, they drove on carrying the last eye-witness news of our progress back to the doubting Thomases of Keith. I didn't know it then, but chance meetings with acquaintances in isolated places would be commonplace in a country with a population of only 10 million.

Next a fisherman with his wife and four children had squeezed us into their new Toyota. When the kids discovered that I was a real American, the first they'd ever seen, they were all eyes and ears and couldn't keep their hands off me. The family overwhelmed me with questions, wanted to show us everything, bought us cokes and urged us to come to dinner. After stopping frequently to show us off to a few of the locals, they were kind enough to drive us all the way back to Standsbury and our first driver who whisked us back to Port Wakefield.

The Barkers of Port Wakefield immediately ushered us, two strangers, into their home. As soon as she realized I boarded with their friends, the Groves in Keith, Mrs. Barker beamed, "Of course you must stay the night." A warm fire blazed, coffee was brewed, Mrs. Barker brought out the first of her quantities of delectable homemade biscuits* and we spent the evening enthusiastically exchanging witticisms and information. The Barkers so simply and warmly welcomed us, unquestioningly offering their all--house, food, time, friendliness, as if it was the most natural thing to do. And it was.

The second day flew by. Mrs. Barker bundled us off into the fleeting clouds and rain squalls with repeated invitations to stop in on our way home. Several short lifts later, in the harbor and industrial town of Port Pirie, a young couple picked us up. We were only an hour away from Port Augusta, but they convinced us that it was well worth the risk of departing the main highway in order to take the back and scenic route.

That was how we came to be sitting on our rucksacks in the seemingly deserted village of Murray Town where only a handful of buildings made up the main and only street. Placing ourselves in what seemed a strategic position before the dollhouse-sized, but grandly named, Australia and New Zealand Bank, we settled down to wait. And wait. And we shivered. And got hungry. The few vehicles that passed us were going in the wrong direction. We bought packages of biscuits from the only store--and what appeared to be the only people in the town. As we waited, we munched biscuits and grew sillier and colder. Finally, for diversity, we moved up the road and leaned ourselves and our sacks against a large yellow road sign which had CHILDREN printed in bold black letters on it. Along came a car. Quickly we hid our biscuits, not wanting the driver to think we were so affluent as to actually have food. Whether it was our sorry-looking countenances or the implied appeal of the children sign, the car stopped.

Our ride was a hitchhiker's dream, a lonely salesman of Russian extraction, who was eager to go out of the way to show us as many sights as he could. He represented the essence of why hitchhiking is so satisfying both to driver and rider. By helping us achieve our freedom, he became a participant in it, vicariously satisfying his own yearnings to wander.

With our assent, he detoured up the windy road to the Alligator Gorge National Park. There we walked along the dry, red creek bed awed by the lofty ruggedness of the russet rock walls pushing in on the narrow serpentine gorge.

On our way again, our driver urged, "You ought to see Whyalla. It's only 30 miles beyond Port Augusta. I could get you back to the airport easily by ten o'clock tomorrow morning."

More back seat consultations. We were pleased for the opportunity to see the famous ship building yards and the gigantic iron works of Whyalla. Consulting her address book to see if she knew anybody there, Gladys came up with the name of an old schoolmate at teacher's college. She rang Jane from a phone box and in a conversation, conspicuous for its honesty if not for its tact, she explained, "We just arrived in Whyalla. We didn't know anyone else to ring so we rang you."

Jane's family gallantly invited us to spend the night with them. Warm showers, a hot meal, our own beds, all appeared as we were welcomed into their fold, already swollen by two house guests--one of them a young girl from Keith. There was even a piano, which I was avidly encouraged to play. Here, as with every family I've stayed with, the household delighted in having their piano in use and in listening or singing along with the music. No one cared that I made mistakes or stopped or had to start over. They loved the gift of the music and I loved being the vehicle for it. Glad and I also, as usual, made ourselves useful with the dishes and the clean-up, enjoying the friendly banter and chatter that accompanied it. We loved the camaraderie, the excitement, and of course we were full of anticipation of the next day when we would fly to Coober Pedy.

*   *   *

Now we sat at the Port Augusta air strip, Eric having flown in and out while we were in town phoning Adelaide to find out where he was. Munching our jelly beans we discussed our options. Should we push on despite the road conditions and our need to be in the Keith classroom next Monday? Could we really hitch up and back in a week?

The airfield caretaker obligingly ferried us out to the "highway," a two lane, deserted road, promising to return for us later, should we still be there. Our wait was enlivened by the local policeman dropping by. He offered little assistance aside from taking our names so as to send out search parties should we not arrive in Coober Pedy by Thursday. After a while, a man on a grader clattered up and assured us that we could have a lift north the next morning with him and the Highways Department Transport. Ecstasy! Jubilation! We hopped up and down laughing and chattering, stopping short when we suddenly realized that we were being observed from across the road by a clan of Aborigines. Where they appeared from, we had no idea.

After our dismal failure of the morning, we were now invigorated and revitalized by our new course of actually achieving Coober Pedy under the most difficult conditions. After all *anybody* could travel by plane, but to venture by road required real grit.

That evening we were taken in by the kind airfield caretaker, who fed us and deposited us back on the road early the next morning. Within ten minutes we were picked up by a convoy of three yellow trucks heading to Coober Pedy. Only after a half day's travel did we discover that this wasn't the expected lift promised the previous day. No matter; as guests of the Australian Geological Survey, we were in excellent hands. Our convoy consisted of two large trucks and a Land Rover towing a trailer. Gladys and I were assigned the passenger seats in each of the large trucks.

The road was like a high dike traversing a red ocean of desert. All day we pushed along, our sole stops being to pull out several bogged down trucks or to bludge a beer from the numerous overturned beer semis that wallowed like beached whales in the thick gummy mud.

Kingoonya, the only community we passed, was a handful of houses, some natives, a pub, and no camera film, but we and our three escorts enjoyed lunch and laughter there. Shortly up the track mini-disaster struck when my vehicle suddenly died. For an hour and a half Glad and I lounged alongside the track nibbling jelly beans and reading until the men revived the truck.

That afternoon's drive found us only 80 miles north of Kingoonya. After a couple of conferences, it was decided to pull off the road for the night. Like a wagon train we followed each other into a cluster. Our escorts, Ian, Jim and Pete, considerately served us tea (dinner) and set us up with Geological Survey stretchers and blankets, never once making us feel uncomfortable about being the only females in their presence. Circling ourselves around the fire we settled in for the night, gazing up at a far-flung sprinkling of glittering stars.

The cold set in. It was, as Jim so graciously put it, "Ten past bloody three," when Glad satisfied all of our various silent wishes and built up the fire again. Our blankets were soaked through from the dew and I dug down deep in my sleeping bag. But it was no use. Eventually we all stirred and the camp became a bevy of motion, packing up, roasting crumpets, "dressing", or rather peeling off the layers of clothes we'd worn to bed.

Our convoy rolled out early, stirring up the dust in three streams as we trundled on, one behind the other. The Land Rover led, unable to set as good a pace as the bigger vehicles, but he was placed there as a precaution should his troublesome petrol tank act up. I appreciated the luck Glad and I had to fall in with this group and the necessity of traveling in two or three vehicle caravans. We would have been hours stuck on the road the previous day had the larger truck not been there to set us going again.

This indeed was the Outback. The country in that overcast, cold morning was somewhat like I imagined Siberia to be--absolutely barren, stretching for vast, flat miles like an endless sea of dull, brackish scrub mottling the red soil. Along the sides of the track

This indeed was the Outback. The country in that overcast, cold morning was somewhat like I imagined Siberia to be--absolutely barren, stretching for vast, flat miles like an endless sea of dull, brackish scrub mottling the red soil. Along the sides of the track glimmered a thin layer of intense green, the result of the rare occurrence of torrential rains the week before. I was sure the landscape would be twice as formidable and bleak without that added attraction of color. How glad I was to be doing this journey in May, and not in the summer. Granted, I was cold and sat bundled in layers of clothing, but what a glaring, searing, God-forsaken waste this land would be in the heat of the summer months.

The frequency with which we jolted over stock grids surprised me. It was difficult to picture people really eeking out a living in that land. But we did see the occasional station or a road presumably leading off to one. Suddenly we stopped before a phenomenal sight, a huge "lake" stretching across the road. Disappointed, we turned about, retracing our track to the fork where we'd decided that this was the safer route, since it was labeled a "Wet Weather Road" on the map. Back we bounced over the rocky, barren, pitted track, through the same grayish, scrubby bushes cropping stubbornly out of the red soil, past the twisted, stunted, more dead than alive looking trees, their black, naked limbs grotesquely reaching out in agonizing gestures.

We turned down the "Dry Weather Road." It must have been, too, for there were many muddy spots which required clever maneuvering. Then ahead of us we could see the left trailer tire behind the Land Rover smoking and looking quite flat. After a mad mile of waving and tooting horns, we finally got the driver's attention. While the men had the thankless task of changing the tire in the bitter cold wind, Glad and I chattered snug and warm in the cab of my truck.

Within minutes of resuming our journey, it was discovered that the spring of the trailer was also broken. Once more we turned around, driving back to the last airstrip where the trailer was abandoned. There was another conference and the men decided that the original road was the correct one, and we should have gone straight through the water in the first place. So once more we retraced our tracks.

mile, until one mile number turned over and, without any fanfare, we stopped--out of petrol. The barren open horizon alone accompanied us and not a bloody bush was in sight. It was under just such circumstances that I learned to dispense with the details of false modesty. I simply went around the back of the truck.

The others rescued us and soon we were in Coober Pedy, camped in the big truck with our escorts who looked after us honorably. We all lay piled up in the cavernous truck swathed in sleeping bags and bundles of Geological Survey blankets, joking, laughing and bantering far into the night.

The next morning found Glad and me standing alone on the road, and our protectors disappearing up the hill on their journey to Alice Springs. We'd made it. Our first business was to look Coober Pedy over--and to find a way of leaving.

Coober Pedy was a handful of wooden and corrugated metal structures squatting in the middle of a vast parking lot-sized swath of road cut through the red rock of a flatish hillside. Beyond the few utilitarian buildings--a general store, gas stations, mining supplies, machine shop, pub--wooden doors pockmarked the red hillsides. A double-sized pockmark with a cross on it designated the church. People slipped and slid their way along the main street, which was a mass of gooey red gumbo.

The general store became our headquarters. Here we saw and were seen by every person in Coober Pedy. Here, too, we struck up conversations with curious miners and noted the fascinating sociological composition of the place. In this bleak, barren outpost a cosmopolitan community was gathered representing nearly every country in the world. There were many different and interesting men, and conversations and questions flowed.

Johnny the Greek offered to take us to an opal mine. Trusting his intentions, we drove with him out across the flat, red rubbly horizon, passing heaping piles of mine diggings, and finally stopping adjacent to the rim of a gaping dark hole. Beside it the five Italian owners of the mine huddled around a fire. Glad and I were each in turn strapped into a harness and lowered down the shaft. At first we hesitated, but once down in the mine, we were at ease in the confidence of our little Italian guide. The long cave was pleasantly warm and quite homey, strung as it was with many dangling salamis and cheeses, which we enjoyed sampling despite the half inch layers of mold that were scraped off of them. Our hosts gave us picks and we pecked at traces in the rocks, coming away with a few handfuls of colorful potch ("almost" opals).

What a life they led, these men surrounded by heaps of gravel, and living in hovels or shacks. For many of them it was a good life. Just sink a shaft, stake a claim and dig. Most of them found it easy to stay for years.

Back at our headquarters, the beer truckers who had gratefully loaded our Geological convoy down with beers after we'd pulled them from the muck of the track were trickling in. Glad and I delightedly ran up and greeted them conversing as with old friends. That night we were their honored guests, "shouted" by all of them to a fish and chip dinner. The remainder of the evening was spent being escorted from one group of miners to another, with Glad and me usually being the only females present. Around midnight we were given space on the floor of a dugout, after first being persuaded to postpone our planned departure so we could be around for somebody's 21st birthday the following night.

The next day we were treated to the sight of some household expansion. The men had decided they needed another room in their quarters, so they simply set their dynamite and blew out another piece of hillside.

At 5 a.m. the following day, we left Coober Pedy on the most fantastic travel conveyance I've ever encountered. Our ride was a Mack truck with a semi-trailer. Atop the flatbed of its trailer was the semi-trailer of another Mack truck being transported back to Adelaide for repairs. Perched on top of the second flatbed was its cab. We roared off, with me crammed in the downstairs cab with the diminutive driver, Gulio, and his eight year old son, Dino, while Brian, the owner of the piggyback truck, and Gladys sailed along aloft in its high cab.

Ever so slowly we lurched along the dirt road, our ship of the desert swaying like a drunken camel. At Mt. Eba we detoured off the track long enough for Gulio to take on a cargo of kangaroo carcasses, shot by locals and destined to become dog food in the city. We only had to stop once to pull out a bogged down semi.

Trading places with Glad after Kingoonya, it was my turn to sway and lurch in the lofty cab of the second semi. Even with the constant swaying and dipping I managed to sleep after Brian stretched himself out over me so as to keep me from bouncing off the seat. Sometime later, a mighty crashing woke me. Our overhigh ship was demolishing the tree limbs and power lines of Port Augusta. The plans for resting and sleeping there quickly changed as Gulio decided he preferred to continue driving rather than risk the legal repercussions for having blacked out the town's power.

Rocks bouncing on the window of my high cab awakened me the next morning. We were in a truck yard in Adelaide, having just arrived after a 24 hour drive for Gulio. I was sorry to depart our perch, sorry to see our ship of the desert dismantled as the cranes lifted first the cab and then the trailer off the back of the Mack. I was sorry to have to say good-by to our friends, to be dropped back where I'd begun, at a bus stop in Adelaide. Was it possible that all this had happened and we merely came back to a bus stop? Leaving Gladys at her friend's house, I walked on to my own friend's home, the center of attention in my red, mud-spattered attire and rucksack.

Back in Keith and classes the next day, Glad and I were momentary celebrities who prowled about grinning like Cheshire cats. Certainly we had no lessons planned, and we regaled the children and the teachers with tales of our wondrous adventures. The kids had never been more attentive.

*   *   *

I'd had a taste of the Outback, and its flavor agreed with me. Mostly it sang of the generosity, hardiness and enthusiasm of the many and mixed people who had joined us in our journey. Today the song is different. As Sid and I flashed along the interior's slick, new bitumen road, the efficient and comfort loving part of me welcomed today's ease, while the adventurer part inwardly sighed and died a little. Of course, "progress" is inevitable, and often wonderful, but how lucky I've been to have had it both ways.

COOBER PEDY 1990

WE GRACIOUSLY SPOONED our way through the mango cheese cake and fresh strawberries with bavaroix creme anglais. An elegant maitre d' had seated us, flourishing napkins onto our laps. A suave grey-suited Italian man cleared our plates. Dinner chatter sifted from the grey clothed tables fanning across the rose-carpeted room. Tall glass blocks and pale pink brick walls alternated with long softly-draped windows, through which glimmered yellowy-orange globs of sparse lights in the desert night.

This was Coober Pedy--1990. Sid and I delightedly contrasted this day's anniversary with those of the two previous years. We loved the exotic, far-flung flavor, from 1988's goat house on Oregon's Sandy River to 1989 at the Cross Roads Condominium of Carmel with spa, pool, VCR and spectacular coastline. Now we'd crossed 535 km of gipper dry desert into the interior of Australia to this fabled mining outpost.

It was a two-fold odyssey. First was the contrast with the two prior years. Second was the strange rhythm that had revolved me back to Coober Pedy after 22 years. Now I arrived as a mature woman, accompanied by the man of my life, able to afford my private caravan park cabin. My computer paraphernalia and financial portfolio littered our comfortable car, and I was sampling kangaroo fillets and Camembert chicken in the sumptuous Desert Cave Hotel.

We were six hours driving the 535 km from Port Augusta. In 1968 it had taken a convoy of trucks two days. Today the country looked less bleak, perhaps because we whizzed so quickly past? I didn't study the tangled, twisted trees as closely, or see them so individually as I once did. Although there seemed to be more green shrubby trees, the same expanse of grey, rugged, desert ground cover prevailed. In the south we saw green, apparently rain-provoked grass, and several vistas of salt lakes and red pyramid peaks. I didn't remember those exotic scenes.

Funny how odd links will make such a difference in an experience. Because I wandered into the Outback Experience Shop in Adelaide and chatted with the friendly proprietor, our way was smoothly paved. I'd phoned ahead to the Stuart Range Caravan Park. When we arrived, John, the Greek owner said, "If you hadn't mentioned Dennis's name, I wouldn't have taken your booking. I always require a deposit." He was completely booked, as was every other lodging during the three weeks of the school holidays.

We had a comfortable brick cabin at $30 a night, a fridge and sink, but no cooking facilities or utensils. Behind the big, spanking-clean office and deli, glittered a richly appointed opal room in which John and his mining partners sold their beautifully mounted opal jewelry.

In regard to the paved road completed four years ago, John said, "I like it. Before, when it rained we had no bread, no milk, no mail."

"Has it made a difference in the tourists?"

"We used to get more tourist busses. Much less now. People come in their own cars."

In a town famous for its underground dwellings, we were disappointed to see so many standard square fibro and cement buildings. We later learned that some claustrophobia-suffering inhabitants prefer above-ground dwellings, and their air conditioning bill is five times that of those in dugouts. The main street had typical, contemporary utilitarian cinder block and tin buildings, most of them garishly emblazoned with signs like: CUT-RATE OPALS; SILLY STONES; CHEAPA TOURS; SEE A MINER'S DUGOUT.

Dust flew up from passing vehicles. Parka-clad tourists peered in and out of shops. Pockmarked with dugout entries which once dominated the town's main street, the hillside was now merely a backdrop to the busy scattering of conventional structures. Beyond the ugly edifices and dusty littered hills, barren desert stretched toward each horizon. To the west, we could see miles upon flat miles of upturned white earth, as if a baker kept overturning funnels of flour. Each of the thousands of pyramids of slag indicated a mine shaft.

Reigning over Coober Pedy's central main street was the modern Desert Cave Hotel. Tall brick, glass and bronze walls fitted nicely into a hillside. We entered the plush lobby and descended pale terra cotta tile stairs to the catacombs below. Long hallways had been excavated just like a dugout or mine. Informative and attractive displays related Coober Pedy's history and explained the mining procedures.

Eighty percent of the world's opals come from Coober Pedy. For $25 one can buy a miners right, good for one year. Anyone can mine, or noodle, or fossick. For the benefit of forgetful patrons, the local drive-in runs an ad: NO EXPLOSIVES ALLOWED IN THIS THEATER. I imagine the advent of the tourist era has initiated new issues for the miners, for many displays explained in great detail how to be careful in the mining fields. Don't let children wander. Don't walk backwards with a camera.

Mine shafts, Coober Pedy.

On the second day we did George's tour. (Again, thanks to my moments with Dennis at the Outback Experience shop.) Every seat of George's rainbow painted bus was filled. As we bounced along, George, speaking in his Dutch accent, regaled us with his buoyant personality and jokes. We learned that Coober Pedy lies 1800 feet above sea level. It maintains a "floating" population of 4,000. There are 41 opal shops and 47 nations represented. The two largest groups are Greeks and Yugoslavs. Food supplies arrive twice a week.

The name Coober Pedy derives from the aboriginal term "Kupa Piti" meaning "white man living in hole." Coober Pedy is in the driest section of the driest state on the driest continent. The average annual rainfall is three to five inches. In 1989, records were broken when 25 inches of rain fell. Nearby Lake Gibson for once was filled with water, and the enterprising locals formed a yacht club which lasted as long as the water did--about ten months.

George told us that the cost of a miner's right had gone up to $28. For that you stake a 150 x 150 foot claim by driving in four pegs. We learned that Coober Pedy was running out of underground hillsides and that folks were moving to the suburbs. We rattled through a cluster of hills where excavations were in progress. On one hill a free lighter--windlight--charged batteries and provided electricity. It was the last of its kind in Coober Pedy. Just in front of it, electricity workers busily installed a power pole.

Our rainbow painted bus grated to a halt beside a mine. Down we went. Inside, George passed out dowsing rods, encouraging group members to try them. He turned on a black light, showing us how miners can easily detect the gleaming opal in the chalky rock. Next we clattered out to a distant area of rubbly slag heaps. Everyone got out of the bus and noodled (rummaged) in the slag. One lady found an opal.

Back in town, we stood on someone's rooftop next to the TV aerial poking from the ground, and viewed bevies of tin pipes and 40 gallon drums poking out of the opposite hillsides. These were water tanks for the underground houses. George pointed out the banker's "house"--distinguished by its blue-tinged skylights glinting from several spots in the red earth. After visiting the dugout Anglican church, we arrived at the grand finale--George's dugout. Inside, we drank cuppas and clustered around the big table in his modern kitchen or sat in the chairs in his dugout lounge room. Each room was as attractive and well-appointed as in any modern house. They were distinguished, however, by the scraped-looking curved walls and ceilings which were painted a soft white. Paintings and hollowed out spaces for shelves decorated the walls.

On our last morning, as we departed Coober Pedy's ragged and garish main street, I once again realized how precious had been my 1968 experience in that town. I'd touched into the miners' lives at a genuine level. The welcome which they'd extended had nothing to do with attracting tourists or their money or with making a big deal out of the mining lifestyle. In 1990, it seemed that Coober Pedy's rugged personality flourished on tourist dollars and on commercializing itself. Just like the rest of the world.

The lounge room of George's dugout.

THE LARAPINTA TRAIL

I SANK ONTO our host's lounge room couch utterly exhausted, and savored long slow swallows of ice water. My hips felt like swivel sticks. But it was the kind of fatigue I relished, filling me with a sense of accomplishment and gratitude for such a day and for such a healthy, strong body. I'd just hiked seven hours and 22 kilometers on the Larapinta Trail.

The trail, in the heart of Central Australia, currently extends approximately 27 kilometers from the old Telegraph Station at the original Alice Springs, to Simpson's Gap, a spectacular yawn in the midst of soaring red rock cliffs. Sid and I returned there three times to walk on different sections of the track. Each hike was a chance to deepen our relationship with the harsh but beautiful land.

Sometimes we would separate from each other, allowing ourselves the opportunity to walk silently, alone, as if we were the only person in that wild and empty space. The track dipped and climbed and wound along rocky hillsides. As we achieved high ground, ever more scatterings of distant ranges, rims, and bluffs rose into view. Their shapes and colors constantly changed with the sun and the shadows, verging from pale pastels to velvet purples.

Thanks to the May rains, we were hiking through a colorful banquet of vegetation. Vivid green grasses skimpily fringed the red dirt. Magenta succulents, large purple-flowered fleshy clumps, and tiny lobelia-like pinpricks sprinkled the rocky ground. Chest high sagey shrubs profuse with fragrant yellow blossoms intermingled with bushes bearing sparse flowers the color of faded periwinkles. Tiny fuchsia-red pindots sprinkled silver leafed hedges, while overhead scarlet drops dripped amidst dark, burnt looking branches. Sometimes the breeze smelled as pungent as perfume.

On our first day's hike, we started at the much more strenuous Simpson's Gap end of the trail. It snaked up and down and along several ridges and saddles while overhead towered the red rimrock of Rungutjirba Ridge. As we climbed, we gained a distant view of Alice Springs nestled like lumps of cotton amidst the rises of many rocky hillocks. Below sprawled the pale pinks and greens of the wide Larapinta Valley, hemmed in the distance by the red-rimmed Heavitree Ranges that run for miles east and west. Behind Alice Springs the ranges break, forming the famous Gap through which people coming from the south enter the town.

We followed an offshoot trail that led up to Scorpion Spring. There we discovered a tiny pond of amber water surviving in a beautiful swale of jumbled white and red rock, threaded with thin trunked ghost gums, shrubs and grasses. The scorpions at the pool, our handout informed us, were the non-stinging kind.

It is expected that the Larapinta Trail will one day extend for 200 plus kilometers along the MacDonnell Ranges. It will be popular because of its proximity to Alice Springs and because the ranges contain some striking formations. A 170,000 hectare national park is planned for the Western MacDonnells which has seen visitor numbers soar from 90,000 in 1987 to 230,000 by the end of 1990.

The trail is being excavated by local convicts. A recent article explained how the convicts preferred working outdoors on the trail to being in jail. "Low risk" prisoners with sentences of one year or less are selected. Usually they are men convicted for alcohol-related crimes, and they usually are Aborigines.

The trail was beautifully executed, with smooth surfaces, rock steps and drainage areas. Frequent directional, kilometer and places of interest markers coordinated with the explanatory map which we carried. It was essential to carry water, but there were even remote spots where untreated water is provided.

It's so easy for visitors to come to Alice Springs these days and alight from airplanes or tourist busses, promenade the mall and souvenir shops, eat gourmet repasts in four star lounges, and peer from air-conditioned vehicles at the famous surrounding gorges--and remain, all the while, completely uninvolved with the flavor of the land.

For Sid and I, walking the Larapinta Trail was perhaps the most eloquent way for us to catch the feeling of the rugged area around Alice Springs. It brought us into close connection with the land, away from people and habitations, giving us a powerful sense of isolation and space and a tiny taste of what the Aborigines and the early pioneers must have felt. My thanks go out to both the men who conceived and the men who constructed the trail.

A HAPPENING IN ALICE

THE ALICE JUNCTION Tavern in Alice Springs noisily swirled with drinking, smoking, chattering folks. Men with long hair and beards held beers or children. Women in batiks and digger hats smoked and hugged. Aboriginal patterned T-shirts sprinkled the room with color. Aborigines, cleanly and neatly, and even fashionably dressed, sat comfortably rubbing shoulders and drinks with whites. They were such a far cry from the shuffling souls with averted eyes whom one saw on the Alice streets.

Laughing, big-eyed, dark skinned children darted happily among the mixed crowd. These multi-racial and diverse groups might have been Americans, mingling and greeting friends with hugs and smiles--confidant and comfortable with one another.

This was the scene of the benefit concert for The Gap Youth Center. Sid and I had learned about the event in town, but little did we know that we had stumbled on to an incredible event--a happening not often experienced by many Australians, let alone by foreign tourists.

Things were getting underway. A handsome clean-cut Aborigine seemed to be in charge, announcing, leaping on and off the stage, rushing about, directing technicians. Not until later did we learn that he was Ernie Dingo, a famous singer whose name we recognized instantly.

Upon arriving at the tavern, I had been intrigued by a man sitting outside on the patio wearing a blue beret. He was young and sinewy, and the rolled up sleeves of his shirt revealed that his right arm was a hook. I was fascinated because he seemed so obviously unconcerned about camouflaging his prosthesis. Soon, I was to be even more amazed by this man.

Several performers had gathered at the tavern including the well known musical group, *Gondwanaland*. When *Gondwanaland* was announced, the man with the hook for an arm stepped briskly onto the stage. He turned out to be Charlie McMahon, the group's lead performer, and the man responsible for producing the incomparable haunting didgeridoo sounds that soon filled the air.

He stood with legs wide apart front to back, a study of power and concentration. With his right arm (hook) he clutched the didgeridoo. He held it at chest level extending several feet in front of him, its long body cradled in the crotch of a stick attached to a pole. His left arm rhythmically sliced the air as he played for long stretches, doing what is called circular breathing, and coaxing incredibly rich, echolike vibrations from the ancient instrument.

The resonating sounds of the didgeridoo seemed to penetrate through my being, connecting me with some deep, inner primeval identity. After the concert, I acquired a *Gondwanaland* tape. When I listened to it as we were driving across the timeless land, in some mysterious way the deep vibrations seemed to thrust me right into the landscape. The music so perfectly expressed the land: the ever-changing interplay of red rimrocks and lavender ranges; ghost gums and grey shrubs; desert rocks and vast horizons. It was as if the land spoke through the tones of the didgeridoo, embracing and connecting with me on some profound level.

Behind Charlie McMahon the drummer flourished bare palms on a panel of drums. To his left, a third man pounded out synthesized melodies on a keyboard. Sid and I could hardly believe our good luck at being able to see and hear such a fine and unique performance. And this was just the beginning.

After nearly an hour, *Gondwanaland* gave way to singer, Bobby Randall--a chubby, sweet-faced, older Aborigine who sang and played the guitar. He sang *My Brown Skinned Baby, They Take Him Away*, which I had heard on one of the Aboriginal tapes of composer/singer Ted Egan. This was the man who wrote that song!

The next performer, Jimmy Little, had trouble with his electric guitar and while we waited for it to be fixed, Ernie Dingo filled in. He sang for his mother, a large, gentle, but strong-looking, white-haired woman seated at a big center table laughing and chatting animatedly with Ted Egan and other whites. Several children of all ages and colors bobbed around the table.

Eventually it was decided that Jimmy Little's guitar couldn't be fixed and he came on stage with an unamplified guitar. He was an older man, rather stout, with a noble black profile, grey hair and beard, neatly dressed in slacks, sport coat and turquoise shirt.

Charlie McMahon and the didgeridoo.

He had an infectious personality. A richness and strength rang through his mellifluous voice. Starting with crooner songs and ballads, he was soon singing popular sixties rock numbers, songs like *Sweet Sixteen, Personality, Country Roads, The Old Cotton Fields of Home* and many more. His charm was contagious as people quickly followed his invitation to sing along. The music grew more and more electric. Some people just couldn't sit still any longer, but got to their feet to dance on a miniscule strip of floor in front of the stage. Sid and I were thumping our hands and swinging our feet to the beat of the music. We were amazed to learn that Jimmy and the young men backing him on bass, drums, and keyboard had never played together before.

Ted Egan was typical Ted with his "Fosterphone" beer carton and humor and sensitivity. He finished with my favorite, *Sayonara*

183

Nakamura, about the Japanese pearl divers in Broome. Then, another Aborigine, Bart Willoughby--a young man with long hair and a clean-cut look about him, appeared on stage and sang about the Aboriginal Woman: *She's Here to Stay*. He followed this number with faster, more intense, pulsating songs. By then, people were dancing on every available bare inch of floor space.

Suddenly, into the pub strode a wild haired, striking black man wearing long, thin jeans, a denim jacket, and a red shirt. Grinning from ear to ear, he stepped onto the stage as if it were his very own. With brash confidence, he helped himself to a microphone and began clapping sticks and trilling yells. I didn't know who he was, but he seemed at home and known by the crowd. Between songs, he strode energetically among the audience, greeting people and fondly embracing both whites and blacks. To one little boy he gave his autograph.

Not until a few days later when I read a newspaper article on the concert, did we learn that this striking black man was the actor, David Gulpilil. We also found out that unbeknownst to us, the American actor, Sam Neil had been quietly sitting in the audience. He, Ernie, David Gulpilil, and others, were in Alice Springs making the film *Until The End of the World*, and this accounted for the high-powered line-up of performers donating their time to the concert.

Gondwanaland returned to the stage and more intense music filled the room. Charlie McMahon strode across the stage. This time he was sweeping an *amplified* didgeridoo high into the air and down again to the floor in swirling circles followed by forward and backward swings. The dashing black man invited himself back on stage where he crouched low, trilled and beat more sticks. Throughout the tavern, whites and blacks, caught up in the sounds, were pulsing to the primitive, yet contemporary music.

In that place and moment, I felt that I was witnessing the breaking of a shell--and the emergence of a new way of being. Admittedly it was only a small roomful of people. Certainly there were lots of sodden "good 'ol boys" present, looking on, drinking with the mates. But many of these people represented the new Australia--the new world idea that celebrated unity in diversity. They were people who sang or talked or acted on behalf of the environment; people who were comfortable wearing colorful, nonconventional clothes and who allowed themselves to burst into dance or song; people whose reality was honesty.

In that pub, in that music, whites and blacks, equally enraptured, were swept into its pulse, its rhythm and feelings. The parents of these people wouldn't have sat down together. In other places in Alice Springs and across Australia, such a coming together was still far from happening. But it happened there, at that moment, in a magical way.

I felt these singers expressed the very heart of what was happening. All of them were balladeers in the sense that they reflected and expressed the currents of the culture. Before the concert, my Australian heroes had been Ted Egan and John Williamson because they celebrated the country and its diverse peoples, and because they called attention--with sensitivity and humor--to the crimes of the past and present, sounding a call to the population to wake up, listen, act and be aware.

Now I'd seen artists, black and white, united in expressing their love for the land, their hope for an end to separation, their belief in the world as a good place and their commitment to working and singing together for the benefit of all.

And the presence of Charlie McMahon broke another sort of shell. By simply being there, doing what he does, he was an impressive model, both for those who think of themselves as disabled and for those who believe the disabled should hide their disabilities. I loved his casual openness and honesty: Here I am! This is it! This is my hook! He'd thrown off his shirt down to a singlet, revealing the leather shoulder strap and the stump sock, as if it was the most natural, ordinary thing. And lo--it became that.

Before seeing Charlie McMahon, I'd assumed that a prosthesis should be hidden, played down and pretended not to exist. But thanks to his open, revealing manner, I didn't even notice it anymore. It became just another part of his body. I wanted to whip on my hearing aids (which I'd removed because the music was so loud) and stand to be counted with this genuine, independent man.

Years ago when I finally ceased hiding my hearing aids and cut my hair short, it marked a step toward presenting myself as real. Charlie McMahon was the essence of REAL. Not only was he uninhibited about his arm, but he had learned the difficult art of playing the didgeridoo and, by marrying it to contemporary music, he and *Gondwanaland* managed to bring the ancient instrument to modern ears. He spoke of timelessness and the land and gave us a taste of it in his music.

I came away inspired, excited, high and filled with hope, having experienced an afternoon where a small pocket of humanity had been full of spontaneity, joy, fun, harmony, talent and dignity. I saw that change *is* happening. No matter how seemingly insignificant this event may seem to be, it was one indication that we *are* opening to each other and to the land that sustains us. I was excited as I saw this face of Australia and knew that, despite some appearances to the contrary, it was the emerging face.

ULURU

WE WATCHED, A little dismayed, as colorful dots inched up and down a thin grey line over the rock's face. At its base, busses and cars already cluttered the parking area. It was only eight o'clock in the morning and already pilgrims were descending "The Climb" at Uluru, or Ayres Rock. Sid and I joined other newcomers reading cautionary signs in German, English and Japanese, telling us that the climb was 1.6 km round trip--and difficult.

Finally, we could delay no longer and began clambering up the steep slope, gripping the cold, metal chain with our hands and grinning as we met the eyes of other pilgrims. Frequently we sat down to rest and wisecrack and watch ten year olds trot blithely downhill. Whipping wind raced across the narrow ridge. One misstep to either side would send us sprawling straight over the sheer edge toward the earth a hundred feet below.

Thin, scaly craters like water marks afforded a millimeter's grip or toe hold. Some people pulled themselves up the chain using both hands. Others trudged forcefully forth, disdaining assistance. It was the descenders who looked interesting, though. Some sat on their behinds, warily mincing downward, gripping the rock with one hand and the chain with the other. Many turned around and maneuvered themselves backwards.

The place could well have been renamed "Little Japan." Numerous well-groomed Japanese, mostly young, made up the crowd. Slim Japanese girls looking like frail flowers scampered up and down the red rock. And along with them were people of every other nationality, age and shape, sporting high-tech tennies, neon parkas and designer backpacks.

After the last section of the chain, the track broadened and flattened as we followed white paint prints along the undulating upper reaches of the rock. Extensive east-west striated ridges crisscrossed Uluru like lines of red ocean waves. Arriving at the crest of a "wave," we would gingerly inch downward. Sliding on our posteriors was a popular strategy. Near the bottom we would release our leg brakes for a quick downward dash which propelled us a few feet up the opposite "wave." From there we clambered upward, usually utilizing our hands, or if we were lucky, someone might heft us from behind or pull us up from above.

At the cairn at the top of the climb, Sid and I joined the line of people waiting to have their photo taken as they signed the visitors' book. Then we left the chattering clusters of elated pilgrims and sought some moments alone. Taking different routes, we each continued across Uluru's wrinkled red roof. Left and right the long ridges creased like rolls of scrunched-up fabric, curving over the sides into massive draperies plummeting to an unseen base. Pockets of collected water peered darkly from small hollows in the ruts and ridges. Sparse green spreading canopies of scraggly trees cropped out from soil-filled nooks.

Sitting alone, looking out across the dry red creases of rock, I saw --the sea! Pale grey-green scrub dissolved into a distance as flat and blue as an ocean. Miles away, scatterings of pale peaks jutted dimly on the horizon. Always, as we climbed, and again from the top, our constant focal point was the pale pink and lavender formations of Katatjuta (or the Olgas). They clustered like massive upturned eggs, 30 km to the west across the mottled scrub sea. Directly east, in line with Uluru and Katatjuta, was our own familiar landmark from Curtin Springs Station--Mt. Conner. It floated angularly on the horizon like a dark grey battleship.

We rejoined the stream of laughing, chattering tourists descending the roller coaster-like track where most of us sheepishly slid down gullies on all fours. Back at the chain, looking straight down the incline, we gulped. This was it. This was where we marched straight down using our legs for brakes. The chain was slung too low to comfortably bend over and grip it. It was easier to walk upright without assistance, concentrating on keeping the center of balance as low as possible and sitting down often to rest our quaking knees.

Safely at the bottom, our shaky legs gratefully stepped onto flat ground and onto "Center Stage." Gaggles of tourists sat on rings of benches watching the show provided by the rock's climbers. Disembarking or boarding throngs chirped and clustered at the now numerous busses. Many people milled and stood about clicking cameras at us and the entertainment above. In the parking lot, tourists ate sandwiches, hoisted on backpacks, and hung over open car windows exchanging information. We merged into the car park crowd and sank, satisfied, into the seats of our car where we munched snacks and congratulated ourselves.

Later we walked the nine km around Uluru's base, and it was then that the personality of the rock truly resonated. On the climb I'd concentrated on *my* strength or weakness, on pulling out whatever resources *I* could to achieve the top. Once there, it had been hard to take in The Rock. Standing on it, one lost its scale. Everything became a relationship to the horizon, to the scrub sea, to the distant landmarks. Certainly we noticed the climb's steepness, the endless wavy ridges, and gasped at edges plunging down to an unseen base. But the effect was like being on a ship at sea. We roamed its decks, but we couldn't appreciate its bigness.

Now, for the first time I got a sense of the relationship of the rock to the earth and to little me at the bottom of it. With the focus no longer ME, ME, ME, it became THE ROCK, THE ROCK, THE ROCK. And I realized that no photo I'd ever seen had conveyed its character. All the post cards and tourist folders showed the monolith glowing like a neon boat in the setting sun, but it was too isolated and too distant for me to comprehend its immensity and variety. Only at the base, tilting my head nearly over backwards, did I realize what the rock represents.

It is grandeur. Grandeur on the scale of an inverted Grand Canyon. From the pretty, tree dotted, grassy earth I looked up and up the red, smooth sides sweeping down from the massive distant top. Broken-off slabs and slipped-off slices heaped high over our heads. Everywhere the formations amazed me, so different than I'd have guessed from the photos I'd seen in books and on postcards.

Jagged-toothed caverns gapped like huge, open mouths. Cavities of all shapes and sizes pock-marked smooth, red surfaces like holes in Swiss cheese. Black stain streaks ribboned downward. Systems of terraces and bowls and chalices, black streaked, dropped to ancient water holes on the ground. Massive slashes formed sheer walls. High up we could see isolated ecosystems of trees. An immense, long, narrow slab overlaid a rock face like a lengthy handle, with a slice of blue sky sparkling between it and the rock. The rock sometimes looked like a huge, red pudding with striations curving across the top as if shaken out of a mold.

One of Uluru's many caverns.

We came upon Aboriginal sacred sites which were cordoned off. Plaques explained their mythological and ceremonial significance. During the Tjukurpa or creation period, Uluru was shaped into its unique form. This gash in the rock's side was formed when an ancestral being was wounded. An emu spirit imprinted that red wall with its unique pattern.

It's the white man who climbs Uluru. The Aborigines choose not to climb and would prefer that no one climbed it at all. I could imagine that they may feel as Christians might if people entered cathedrals and climbed the altars.

In the same way that individuals might enter a cathedral with awe and respect, could we not do the same here? Even non-religious folks enter a cathedral and speak in hushed voices or not at all. How different would our experience of Uluru be if everyone agreed to walk or climb keeping silence? What would it be like if we could suspend the chatter and distractions so that the focus was only on the rock, the land, the atmosphere--so that we could tune in to what speaks to us and what we are too distracted to hear or notice? What *would* we hear? What would the rock say?

What I heard was man's insignificance. There is very little man can do, short of an atom bomb, to influence or alter that rock. All his chippings and busy-ness are like the labor of ants. Indeed men *looked* like ants, mere specks dotting the climbing slope. Uluru endures and endures and our life spans and efforts are so minuscule beside it. I came away respecting The Rock, the ageless, eternal energy and endlessly enduring process of its creation.

Tune your ear
To all the wordless music of the stars
And to the voice of nature
A thousand unseen hands
Reach down to help you to their peace-crowned heights,
And all the forces of the firmament
Shall fortify your strength.
             Ralph Waldo Trine: In Tune With The Infinite

KATATJUTA

IN THE LONG shadows of early morning, Sid and I embarked on what turned out to be an enchanting journey, a trek into a realm of mystic proportions and spirit. We had come to Katatjuta, also known as the Olgas, a national park 34 km from Uluru (Ayers Rock) smack in the center of Australia. The first half hour was an easy climb up a rock and dirt trail to Katatjuta Lookout. On our left, steep walls of red rock gleamed brilliant in the early sun. Dark pouches, like vertical eye sockets, formed puckery patterns on the rock face. My imagination took me to Egypt's Valley of the Tombs, and I was sure

Katatjuta from Uluru.

spirits must be hovering in these high depressions and caverns. On our right the hulking rock walls loomed black and green-streaked in the murky morning shadow.

The previous day, as we climbed Uluru, Katatjuta had hung like a fairytale city, rose and gold, on the horizon, its beckoning domes our constant focus. Now, a half hour from Uluru's commercialism, crowds and chatter, we easily slipped into the atmosphere of this unique place. The rough, rocky entry road had efficiently thinned out most tourists. Except for the sporadic buzz of scenic air flights, and "G'day's" to a handful of other hikers, we hiked in a rapturous silence.

At the Katatjuta Lookout, we sat on warm rock ledges taking in the vista. Far away, the mottled specks of green and yellow scrub dissolved into a distance as blue and flat as the sea, broken occasionally by tiny pale pyramids or slug-like profiles of purple ranges. Directly before us, nine chocolate red puddings rose from beds of green and grey-green skirts dotted with clumps of yellow spinifex. To our left, a thin line threaded where the trail curved around the base of the nearest and biggest pudding. Some were perfect domes. Some seemed to have slipped to one side or the other, while others had fallen flat. Bands of dark pinches circumvented some puddings, looking like crimps in the sides.

Softly, the notes of Sid's clay flute floated melodically into the clear air. He is no musician but the sounds were magical, made up from the moment, stopping the moment and the scene, and bringing them into a haunting perspective. Under the flute's spell, we were speaking to the domes, the valley, the scrub and the trees; and they silently, eloquently seemed to hear and respond.

Briskly, we descended the trail following the curve of the large pudding, scaled its final rise, and Kaboom! an incredible array of more giant puddings soared in rows across another wide, pale green valley. The domes beckoned and danced, constantly changing colors and shapes, revealing ever more details as we traversed the gentle grassy valley.

Within an hour we were entering the cool, cavernous gap between two of the domes. The Valley of the Winds was, in fact, a ravine of rubble joining the two monoliths. Beyond this passageway, the massive wall of yet a third dome loomed, leaving a tiny blue channel of sky overhead. High on our right, a red wall brilliantly reflected the sun, casting a rosy aura into our chasm. We walked, hushed, on a red path in a rarified atmosphere of red shadows, red rocks, and red boulders. Wiry trunks of lean gums, pale blue Michaelmas daisies, and my white T-shirt all glowed warm red. Sid's flute silkily suffused the serene air.

After sitting long and silently at the top of the rubbly pass, we descended and followed the trail along a narrow, but sunny gorge between more monstrous walls and domes. An hour later, having completed a circle, we were back in our original lovely little valley. We began the return journey, walking soundlessly except for the moments when Sid's flute cast its enchanting spell.

Suddenly I was in a time warp, as if a curtain drew aside from some all-encompassing, timeless perspective. I glimpsed myself walking through that fragrant, grassy, tree-dotted valley at the base of those looming sentinels. I was watching myself walking in the sun with that particular man in that particular place, watching myself in one moment amidst endless moments as if I were glimpsing myself in relation to eternity, and I was the watcher *and* the walker.

Did I speak to you one morning
*   in some distant world away?*
Did you save me from an arrow?
Did you lay me in a grave?
Were we brothers on a journey?
Did you teach me how to run?
Were we broken by the waters?
Did I lie you in the sun?
I dreamed you were a prophet in a meadow,
I dreamed I was mountain in the wind...[1]

The words of John Denver's song seemed made for that moment, melting me into the flavor of those strange, magnetic mountains and that grassy, sun-flecked valley. The lilting incantations of Sid's flute again penetrated the air, ethereally connecting us with that magical

---

[1] *The Wings That Fly Us Home* by John Denver

place. My heart flowed out to the man who would do that, and to the spirit of Katatjuta.

Sid playing his flute on the Katatjuta trail.

CURTIN SPRINGS STATION

PETER SEVERIN AND his American wife, Margot, greeted us from amidst a convivial cluster of tourists and staff chattering at the bar of their little pub. Sid and I had eagerly anticipated this meeting ever since we'd first heard about Curtin Springs Station. Our host in Alice Springs was a mate of Peter's, and he had set the wheels in motion for us to come and stay on this 4000 square km station. In return for helping out, Peter would give us free lodging. Curtin Springs sprawled smack in the Center of Australia, only a 100 km from Uluru (Ayres Rock). Now, after a three hour drive from Alice Springs, we took our first steps into the unique world of Outback life.

Margot, dressed in a comfortable track suit, sat on a stool next to the bar. A slim lady with a kind, rugged face, her hands cupped her ever-present pack of cigarettes. Peter, short, bandy-legged and silver haired with glasses perched on his narrow nose, was friendly and outgoing. He immediately made us feel at home.

The Curtin Springs story might have been much different had the station not been located on the road to Ayres Rock, and had the owners been less versatile. When Peter bought the lease to the property in 1956, and drove in 1500 head of cattle overland, he was just in time for a devastating ten year drought. With his herd dwindled to 200, he looked at his options and branched into new territory. He and his first wife, Dawn, began catering to the increasing influx of tourists, providing petrol, food and lodging and playing a role in the development of tourist bases at Ayers Rock.

"I built Ayers Rock," Peter said with a twinkling eye. "As I was building my place I used to cart the leftover odds and ends of cement into the bush. The hard part was the painting though."

We asked Peter how his twin businesses of tourists and cattle compared.

"Over a span of five years," said Peter, "our income from tourists and cattle would be equal. Sometimes you make lots of money with cattle. Sometimes zero. Tourists are steady. That's what saved the station during the drought years."

Peter installed us in a roomy tin cabin with IN-DOOR LOO AND SHOWER!!! Sid eagerly plunged into helping construct the corrugated iron roof over Peter and Margot's new metal house, while I spent hours walking in the bush or hibernating in the precious privacy of the cabin catching up on tons of writing.

Each day I crossed the roadhouse compound, passed the cages of exotic birds and the chained up dogs, passed the tourists cars and busses and attractive tin cabins. "You never go anywhere without informing someone," I was told. So I adhered to the rule, telling Sid my estimated return time and my projected route before sallying forth along the dirt road. Five minutes after passing the paddock gate, I was as good as miles away.

I'd step into space and isolation--not scary, but profound and welcoming--walking in bright sun and sharp air. Rabbits darted. Swift flying little birds chirped and twittered. Bones turned red. I walked amidst greys and greens of mulgas and cork trees, yellow-speckled wattles and the ever-present spinifex clumps. Piles of dry grey branches littered the ground. Overhead, withered, leafless limbs stretched black and twisted under the pale lid of the sky.

I was fascinated by the spinifex. It had an almost urchin-like appearance with its chubby green mounds, so perkily scattering themselves across the red earth. Its golden grasses fountained forth looking wonderfully rich and abundant. But what a misleading plant. The long grassy fronds were worthless for animals and one unprotected brush against the spiky base was like shooting your limb full of fine needles.

Whenever I came to an incline or to a gap in the trees, I could see the most dynamic landmark of Curtin Springs Station--the hulk of Mt. Conner hovering purple or red on the southern horizon. Its sides dropped straight down like a tablecloth, the top was flat. The wild landscape was cut by a swath of broad red road which beckoned me to follow it. But I always kept my walking to the fence line. Every time I'd reach a fence corner, I'd simply continue around it. There were bulls in the paddock and I took no chances of being stuck in the same 500 acre enclosure. It could be a long way to run to the safety of the closest fence.

On our third day at Curtin Springs, Peter and Margot organized an expedition to the outlying areas of the station. With another visiting couple, we drove for miles over dirt roads checking bores*, cattle and generators, climbing windmills, and admiring the new self-mustering cattle pens being constructed by Ashley, Peter's son and co-partner.

The land revealed itself to us in one of its more soft, endearing moods. The results of May rains were everywhere--in the tiny green tufts in the red dirt, in the spatterings of colorful blossoms on the shrubs and in the patches of miniscule ground flowers shimmering like lavender lakes. The cattle, we were told, fed on the ubiquitous massive shrubbery. And it must be good feed, too, for the cattle we encountered were in excellent condition. We passed the slender, pink-trunked, frilly-leaved bush poplars. They looked like mini versions of the real thing. Peter told us that these trees, though, matured and died within five years.

Curtin Springs Station, Mt. Conner in background.

We stopped at a barbecue "site," an opening in the scrub next to the red dirt road near a windmill. The scene was the epitome of an Aussie barbecue. Canvas chairs were produced from the car. While we sat drinking beer and swatting flies, Peter built a little fire, hauled an iron grill on to it and threw on slabs of thick red steaks and chunks of sausages. Across the fence, several of the station's mousy colored Murray Gray cattle milled and bellowed and gazed curiously at us. Soon it was time to butter a slice of white bread, place our meat selection on it, add a squirt of tomato sauce, and voila--fast, simple and delicious food.

Our outing provided us with a little outback drama as well as a chance to observe Margot's keen mind. On our way to the barbecue site, we had stopped at a bore and observed all the station horses clustered outside some stock pens. Graphic signs of harshness strewed the area--a dingo carcass by the water tank, two camel carcasses in the paddock, a dead cow near the car, and a dead horse at the entry to the pens. Earlier Margot had told us, "The horses are all out bush," meaning that they were roaming free in a 1000 acre paddock. Because they were living like wild horses, I was surprised at how tame they were, coming up to nuzzle us, and allowing us to handle and fondle them.

On our way home from the barbecue, Margot said to Peter, "I think we ought to stop in again at the horses. I have a feeling they're not going into the pens for water because of the dead horse in the gateway." None of the rest of us had thought of that. We detoured back to the pens and found the horses still milling outside the open gate. By means of a rope attached to the jeep, the men hauled away the carcass from its spot near the gateway. Then we all drove the horses toward the opening. Margot's intuition was proven right. The horses skittered away even from the smell where the dead horse had been. Finally a leader broke through the gateway and the rest quickly followed. The horses rushed toward the trough, where snorting, pawing and splashing, they guzzled the water.

During that day we learned more about the station's stickiest issue, which centered around the Aboriginal drinking problem. At age 60-plus, Peter was ready to let Ashley run the station while he relaxed and stuck to the business of hobnobbing with his guests. Now, he willingly expressed to us the frustration of being taken to court four times in the last 18 months over the issue of his liquor license.

In 1962 the Aborigines were granted the same rights as

Australians, including that of drinking alcohol and getting drunk. Like the American Indians, they are genetically ill-prepared to handle liquor. Two weeks before Sid and I arrived there, over a hundred Aborigine women marched on Curtin Springs proclaiming, "Cursed white man drink is killing our race." They wanted roadhouses to stop selling take-out liquor to Aborigines. The unlimited liquor license at Curtin Springs was like a magnet, they said. Their men drove hundreds of kilometers to drink and buy liquor to take back to Aboriginal communities. The men were usually drunk and violent and families were torn apart.

Peter pointed out, "Many of those women buy alcohol from me and are often found drunk at the station. If I didn't sell alcohol, those who drive long distances to buy it from me would just drive longer distances to buy it from someone else. If I don't sell to Aborigines, it's like the old days when I legally couldn't sell to them. Then I was called a racist. The station down the road restricts its liquor sales to Aborigines, and pulls it off it because it is run by Aborigines under the subsidy of the government."

If Peter loses his 33 year-held liquor license, whites, too, will simply take their business 100 km east or west to the two Aboriginal communities of Yulara or Mt. Ebenezer. Peter's loss of his one certain source of income will be their gain. Four times Peter has travelled the nearly 4000 km round trip to Darwin and won his case. But the other side's white lawyers continue to haul him back to court, at taxpayers' expense, seeking to overturn the ruling. Peter told us that he had already spent $60,000 on legal fees. The last time around, the opposition brought in a barrister from Melbourne. Peter had to do the same, since a barrister is a jump above a lawyer, and you have to be equal. The barrister cost Peter $5000 a day.

The alcohol situation in the Northern Territory is terrible. Alice Springs headlines blared that Alice drinks much more than the national average and consumes a huge number of liters of alcohol a day per person. But how to deal with it. One of the staff women at Curtin Springs worked for over a year at an Aboriginal settlement. She said, "We had to stay in our houses on payday weekends. It was too dangerous to go outside. It was supposed to be a dry settlement, but men drove 100 km to Alice Springs, and brought back $3 bottles of wine and sold them for $50.

"They're on the dole and they have plenty of money to spend on grog. One of the settlement nurses who'd been there over 20 years said, `The babies I brought into the world are all drunk and deformed. It's too much to bear,' and she finally left the settlement."

Even as he voiced his frustration and asked, "Why me?" Peter was able to say, "But there's other blokes who are worse off. We go out and bring in accident victims. People's cars hit cattle at night. Some are maimed and some die. We come back and say, `Now what was I complaining about?'"

For several years, Peter sold meat to the tourist concessions at Ayres Rock. He slaughtered, packaged and air-delivered his own meat to Yulara (the community at Ayres Rock) or to various Aboriginal settlements. Five years ago that enterprise closed down when the government returned Ayres Rock to the Aborigines. Now the whites lease the park and recreation facilities of Yulara from the Aborigines who receive 33 1/3 percent, and an Adelaide meat firm delivers meat from 1600 km away. Peter sold his plane and is trying to sell the now useless slaughterhouse.

On our last Saturday at Curtin Springs, Peter's daughter-in-law, Nicki, arranged a climb of Mt. Conner. She drove us, a New Zealand couple and Allen, a staff member, out on the long circumventing road in the four wheel drive. How different the mighty bluff looked from the south side. Much more hilly and accessible. The others climbed a low rocky escarpment to watch our progress. We traipsed up and down and around a hillside of needling spinifex, following narrow ribbons of rocky animal paths. Then we started the arduous ascent of the water course, which soon became a straight up proposition, with us bounding up and up the red boulders in the morning shade. My energy was wonderful.

At the top, we discovered that what had looked like one linear plateau really contained several branches. Crossing to the long, major arm we looked down. For untold miles we saw grey haze broken by, of all things, silver lakes to the north east. Curtin Springs homestead and the Lassiter Highway were invisible, lost in the boundless expanse. Ever so tiny, about the size of a slug on the western horizon, sat a pale grey Ayres Rock.

We made it. But the others were waiting, so we hurriedly retraced our steps across the plateaus and scrambled down the ravine. We scampered across the spinifex hillside and down the rocky incline to where the others sat in the shade visiting and swatting flies. Back we drove to the thatched roof lean-to by the dam and stirred up a barbecue. From the swale, where the dam water was, came the loud bellowing of bulls. Allen said, "It's because there's too many bulls. They sort of get more aggressive when there's more."

Each evening at Curtin Springs, we all ate in the family style dining room, tourists and staff serving themselves from heaping platters on the huge range. There was always someone new at the table. Many diners were well known to the staff: the fuel truck driver who spends the night once a week, the travelling merchant who drives and sells his bus load of goods to outback communities, tour bus drivers.

Early in our visit the nine staff members were polite but remote, wary of two more strangers dropping into their midst. With each day we observed more of the frustrations of running a roadhouse. Demanding, imperious tourists. Clusters of drunk Aborigines cajoling for more booze. There were endless tasks to be done, and staff members, as well as willing visitors, pitched in to help out. Normally, Ashley lived at an outstation maintaining bores, fences and cattle. When he was at the station proper, he slipped into numerous roles. Among other things, he kept the books, prepared tourist promotions, tended bar, mopped floors, maintained machinery, cleaned cabins, hung out the clothes, and even cooked delicious meals during the cook's days off.

The staff, as loyal mimics of Peter and Ashley, were able to step into each other's places, as unexpected situations were always expected. Periodically they had to drop whatever they were doing and race to rescue travellers who had hit a beast at night, retrieve them from their crushed cars and get them onto a flight out. (The cattle wandered free since it would cost $1000 a km to fence the roadside paddocks, which are 35 km long on each side of the road.) It made for hard work, long hours, and versatility--although sometimes it got to be too much for them, as we discovered one day when Sid came back from the dining room saying, "There's no breaky this morning. The cook got drunk last night."

Gradually the barriers came down. The staff opened up and involved us in their conversations and, with the final days, some more personal sharing took place. So that when the time neared for us to leave, we were reluctant. We felt that we'd just begun to enter into the rhythm and swing of the place, to be received at a deeper level, and to have a strong sense of welcome and acceptance. We left just as we were starting to forge some bonds and to open the doors on friendships with members of this little band.

We had glimpsed station as well as roadhouse life, seeing up close the size, mechanics, legal issues, PR, logistics, etc. that these people dealt with. It was that ability to orchestrate two symphonies at once that impressed me. How many resort managers, I wonder, could run a station? And we'd touched on the people of Curtin Springs, people who came to the Northern Territory for a month and stayed a year or who came for a year and stayed several. What did they come for? "People," said one girl. Yes, a certain kind of people.

People like Michelle, who once drove tourist busses and who dreams of going to Western Australia to work in the mines. And Magda who once ran a women's shelter in the city. She was on her way to Darwin and wound up at Curtin Springs as the invaluable bookkeeper. People like sixty year old Allen, who once broke his neck, but is determined to continue participating in work projects. Allen's passion is land yacht racing. One day he set up his land yacht in the roadhouse compound for us to try, and provided desert travellers with probably the most startling sight of their journey. Approaching Curtin Springs they would have seen a bright white sail skimming incongruously above the miles of scrub, outlined against the red hulk of Mt. Conner.

It's people like Margot who look behind the appearance of normalcy and know what must be done. People like Ashley who can shift back and forth from station owner to roadhouse manager several times a day. People like Peter who even in his sixties, continues to fight for his way of life. They are people who are not afraid of hard work, who are not put off by dirt or dust or difficult conditions and having to make do. Something calls, and they respond to an unremitting land.

Even Peter's dog was waiting at our door the day of our departure, following us into the cabin or out to the car. The dog and I had become fast friends and my heart tore a little as she looked wonderingly at us leaving her behind. There ensued a flurry of warm hugs and goodbyes, exchanges of addresses and promises to keep in touch, and soon the 1000 acre paddocks, the lush, harsh bush and the hard working little colony receded further and further into the distance.

As we drove away from Curtin Springs following the road south, the lovely, severe land splashed a colorful farewell. It looked surprisingly gentle cloaked in yellows upon yellows of shrubby wattles and cheerily colorful white, lavender, purple and red blooms. We passed the red rocks and outcroppings of the Center for the last time--for until how long?--and approached each roadhouse with a new appreciation of all that stands behind it.

THE BALLADEERS

SID AND I fell in love with the music of John Williamson and Ted Egan, two of Australia's best-known balladeers. Both sing about their country, its heart, people and important issues, in a way that captures the imagination and appeals to the sensitivity of listeners.

We first heard of John Williamson when children of friends played his tapes and danced to the rollicking melodies in their lounge room. With delight, I realized that the lyrics depicted places we'd visited. One song was about Broome. Another one, *Sail The Nullarbor*, urged Easterners to cross the continent and experience the wonders of Western Australia:

> *I saw the color changes from Albany to Broome,*
> *a pair of white Corellas* singing out of tune,*
> *wild flowers in bloom,*
> *and I saw the rusty Hamersleys from a dusty Wittenoom.*

Soon after our first encounter with his music, we saw John Williamson perform on television. He was singing the rousing *Rip Rip Woodchip* (about saving the forests) to the spectators at a nationally televised Big League footy* game. I was thrilled. Because die-hard footy blokes and beer boozers, who rarely thought about ecological responsibilities, were listening to a stirring expression of environmental awareness.

After we had bought our own John Williamson tapes, we listened to them by the hour. John's voice has a low-key, laid-back quality that gives the impression that he must be a very likable guy. We found out that John grew up in a rural area and attended a private boys' school in Melbourne. Among other things, he had been a wheat farmer and had been lambasted by timber men for his song *Rip Rip Woodchip*.

Some songs, like *Boogie With M' Baby* and *My Dad Snores* commented humorously on the frailties and foibles of mankind, while others echoed John's deep involvement with the country-- songs about truckies' wives, miners and parched towns praying for rain. One song, *The Drover's Boy*, eloquently expressed the Aboriginal experience when, during the early years of settlement, the women became "drovers boys" after their tribes were massacred.

Wherever we were, whatever we were doing, John's music was the perfect accompaniment for our activities. The songs were alive, fresh and colorful. They brought the flavor of the country into our caravan or cottage, or into the car as we sailed down tree tunneled roads, through little hamlets or past vast farmlands.

When we lived on our friends' sheep farm, I used to walk across fields dotted with sheep and magnificent gums, hearing the call of magpies. I'd think then of the inspiring lyrics to *The March For Australia*, which John wrote for Australia's bicentennial:

> *So fair dinkums* make a stand,*
> *Time to love an ancient land,*
> *Save the bush and save the sand,*
> *Our children will understand...*
>
> *And I'll see the colors with my eyes,*
> *All the wonders will surprise,*
> *From the oceans to the inland skies,*
> *I'll show the world our paradise.*

Later, when Sid and I were staying at Curtin Springs Station in the arid Center, one particular song seemed to give expression to the feelings I had for the place. I loved to walk alone on the rusty red track out from the station buildings. The desert-like bush was just coming alive from the rains of two months before. Flowers in reds, yellows, blues and pinks spattered the grey-green scrub and the massive shrubbery. Others spread like lavender carpets over patches of the red earth. The cobalt canopy of sky simmered overhead. The words of John's most moving song, *Shelter*, written by Eric Bogle, would penetrate those moments, bringing tears to my eyes:

> *And you're drowning in the sunshine*
> *As it pours down from the sky*
> *And there's something stirring in your heart*
> *Bright colors fill your eyes*

As from here to the far horizon
Your beauty does unfold
And oh, you look so lovely
Dressed in green and gold.

Sid and I first encountered Ted Egan at a concert which he gave in Naracoorte. We had no idea what to expect, since the friends who took us to the concert only told us that Ted was famous for accompanying himself on a beer carton. What a wonderful surprise Ted turned out to be. He had a quick wit and repartee, a rich tenor voice, and yes! the beer carton, Fosters Lager XXX, on which he tapped rhythmically with his palms, actually sounded good.

After he'd played some lighthearted, rollicking songs accompanied by his beer carton, or "Fosterphone," Ted said, "My next song, *The Drover's Boy*, won the Australian Heritage award as sung by John Williamson." I'd had no idea that this beer carton playing balladeer was the genius behind *The Drover's Boy*.

Ted told us how a trip to Broome and a visit to the Japanese pearl divers' cemetery had inspired him to write the hauntingly beautiful song, *Sayonara Nakamura*. His eyes sought his wife's across the crowded room and he asked her to sing with him. She responded with softly harmonizing the simple message of farewell and sadness:

So it's goodbye now, farewell,
Say goodbye to Okinawa,
For today they'll bury you in West Australia,
And you will never be as one
With the land of the rising sun,
Sayonara, Sayonara, Nakamura.

Balladeer, song writer, performer, Ted Egan, is a man with a checkered background. He has taught school, mined, and farmed. He has lived and worked among Aboriginal groups and speaks two of their languages. He mentioned to us that he was midway through compiling a ten volume series of song-music-history books and tapes about Australia. These included volumes on shearers and drovers, Anzacs (World War I soldiers), convicts, settlers and Aborigines.

I bought two tapes *(The Anzacs* and *The Aborigines)* at the concert. When I listened to them, I marveled at the depth and breadth of Ted's song writing talent. Like the authentic storyteller

Ted Egan and his "Fosterphone."

he is, his songs, whether haunting or humorous, captured diverse facets of the country's character. His courage impressed me, too. I wondered how well white Australians had received his Aboriginal tape with its poignant honesty.

Both John and Ted inspire my admiration. They have the ability to movingly depict Australia's diverse cultural heritage, the plight of the environment, and underdogs such as dingoes and Aborigines. Their moving messages, straight from their hearts, have reached thousands of people. What I find particularly appealing is how John and Ted adroitly snare "Joe-bloke" listeners in their bouncy web of rollicking drinking, trucker or drover songs. Then, ever-so subtly, they slip in something deep and poignant--to which Joe Bloke would never have listened had he not already been caught up by the enthusiasm of the other songs.

Sid and I wanted to share these ingenious songs, since the Australia we love is also the Australia which John and Ted sing about. Nothing, we felt, could better portray the Australian experience for our friends at home. We bought bundles of tapes and sent them to friends all over the United States. Needless to say, our friends loved the music. They said that they had never seen Australia in such a light, and they wanted to hop on the next plane Down Under.

THE GOURMET CLASSIC

TWENTY MINUTES FROM Gawler, in South Australia's famous Barossa Valley, Sid and I pulled into the Burge Family Winery at Lyndock. It was ten o'clock in the morning and already we were glad we'd come. For the first time in five days the sky was blue, the sun bright. Almond blossoms splashed soft pink or white against the sky, and yellow wild flowers spilled like a tide across oceans of vivid green fields. Quaint Germanic hamlets sparkled festively. The vines, the heart and reason for the life of this valley and for today's event, stood naked, gnarled and brown, unperturbed by nature's and man's festivities.

This was the first day of the Barossa Gourmet Classic, a weekend dedicated to showcasing gourmet food, top class musicians and exemplary wine. For $2 we each bought our souvenir wine glasses. These were immediately filled with samples of the famous local wine. Inside Burge's big white marquee, several long tables and chairs were arranged in rows. Pungent aromas floated from an annex marquee where the white-capped and aproned chefs of an Adelaide specialty restaurant busily prepared tantalizing platters of gourmet food.

Once we were savouring the satay beef and jasmine rice, we realized our mistake. With several hours' eating ahead of us, we should have ordered one plate between us in order to enjoy more variety throughout the day. As we ate, we listened to Rick Peterson on the guitar singing folk, blues and ballads. Sid learned that Rick and others would be performing there that night.

We asked one of the staff, "Can we come?"

"We're booked out."

"Do you think other wineries might have space?"

"Every other nighttime event is booked out too."

Seeing our disappointment, he added, "But since you talk funny, we'll find a way to squeeze you in. It's $12, and you'll get a meal, the entertainment and wine."

"We'd heard that there were evening events, but could find nothing about them in the papers."

He explained, "We never advertise. It gets too crowded."

Elated, we departed Burge's and followed our Classic Gourmet program map to Orlando Winery, where swing music wafted out of cool, cavernous vat-filled rooms. Joining the boisterous crowd, we once again filled our wine glasses. As we did so, we noticed people wearing leather "necklaces". These incorporated leather pouches in which one could place a wine glass for easy carrying between fills.

Minutes down the road, at the Krondorf Winery, we found a green and white marquee, white-clothed tables graced with pink flowers, and The Krondorf Jazz Band. Here we joined the spectators merrily singing along to harmonious renditions of old favorites like *Daisy, Daisy* and *You Are My Sunshine*.

Our route next took us to Rockford Winery, one of the highlights of the day. Crowded tables strewed a gravel courtyard set amidst structures of old-style rock walls, flagstones and tin roofs. (We later learned that these had been created by a renowned "instant ruin" specialist.) Huge wooden vats filled with gigantic flower arrangements stood throughout the yard, and sheaves of wheat were attractively gathered around verandah posts and fence railings. Acacia blossoms flashed yellow splashes against grey stone and dark shadows. Servings of delectable gourmet food flitted on staff-bourn platters across the colorful and chatter-filled courtyard.

Beneath the tin eves of a rock walled shed, The Irish Colonial Bush Band sawed enthusiastically on fiddles, banjos, flutes and mouth organs. With our refilled wine glasses, Sid and I joined the clapping, foot-tapping crowd fervently caught up in the infectious personality, joy and exuberance of the band and their rip roaring music.

Our next stop, St Hallett Winery, offered more wine and a change of pace with its gracious formal atmosphere. A huge 40 foot long shiny mahogany table commanded the marquee's interior. Stylish arrangements of birds of paradise and other exotic flowers graced the table and strategic nooks. At the far end of the marquee, classic strains floated from the instruments of the tuxedo-clad South Australian Wind Quintet. Outside, lawns and tables and flower arrangements drifted down to a hillside brook.

Bush band at the Rockford Winery.

When we arrived at Chateau Dorrien, we hadn't as yet eaten again, and we salivatingly eyed the sumptuously served skewered king prawns and smoked rainbow trout as we listened to *Nite Flyte*. A talented group, all attired in sequined denim, they might have been a family--the father as lead crooner, mum belting into a microphone, elder daughter masterfully "hot" on the electric guitar and younger son and daughter backing up. We bobbed and bounced in our chairs to rousing renditions of songs like *Locomotion, Love Potion Number Nine,* and *Blue Berry Hill.*

Probably the most famous musician at the Classic was James Morrison, known as the Australian Louis Armstrong. After driving and sampling our way up the spring-green valley, we at last encountered James and his Jazz All Stars at the Elderton Winery. A huge crowd spilled out of sprawling twin marquees. There were many empty tables, but it was impossible to sit at one and see the performers, so we joined the clustering throng around the stage.

A slightly rotund, mild looking man wearing a brown plaid suit played a saxophone. Behind him ranged a drummer, bass and piano player. The man was so intensely focused on his music that he seemed oblivious to the crowd--it was just him and the instrument--which he made shriek, slide and shimmer at his command. He was truly a master. In one number, he played and did continuous breathing on and on, until people were roaring and cheering in astonishment and appreciation. Later, as James Morrison introduced songs and band members, his personality came across as friendly, chatty and funny.

As Sid and I listened to the music, we ate again, tempted by the plates of pecan pie swabbed with thick globs of fresh cream, the cholesterol-filled likes of which are totally foreign to American consumers.

In the late afternoon the festivities wound down. In many ways, though, our day was just beginning. Dropping by our friends, John and Margie's farmhouse near Greenoch, we found no one home. Leaving the car in the driveway, we walked along their dirt road, past the neighbor's farm and up the hill where the setting sun streaked shadows across the green fields and trees and fences silhouetted black against the first pink, then orange, horizon.

As we returned down the hillside, a ute approached and stopped. "Are you broken down?" asked the grey haired man at the wheel. Chatting and exchanging names, we quickly learned that this was Greg Martin, John and Margie's neighbor. Greg exclaimed, "*You're* the Yanks John's been telling us about!" Another car, driven by Greg's wife, Stephanie, pulled up. Dressed in boots and jeans, and on her way to feed her hogs and put the piglets away for the night, she took time to join us standing in the darkening road. We all chattered as if we'd known each other for years.

Greg urged, "Come back for a drink. We've got a houseful of guests because of the Gourmet Classic, otherwise we'd offer you our hospitality."

A few moments later we stepped into Greg's long, low, brick house which I'd so often admired during my walks from John and Margie's. Shadows from a blazing fire danced on the white walls of the low-beamed lounge room. Crystals and lights sparkled. Three friendly women stepped forward and drew us immediately into their smiles and conversation. Exchanges and questions and laughter bubbled. Snacks and salmon mousse were urged upon us, and Greg produced a wicker drum of 20 year old Port.

We toured the rambling house appreciating Greg's remodeling of the old building. The low ceilinged, stone-walled rooms reminded me of the Spanish architecture in the American Southwest. Stephanie returned, followed soon by the husbands of the three women. During the day everyone had been out in different directions at the Gourmet Classic.

Warmly drawn into this happy, bright, friendly circle, we felt wonderfully welcomed. We wanted to know each of these intelligent, caring people better. But we'd already paid for the evening's entertainment at the Burge Winery, so reluctantly we said farewell.

Seeing lights at John and Margie's, we stopped and were quickly enfolded in another happy encounter as they and their three guests pulled us into their warm kitchen circle with hugs and laughter and banter. All too soon, though, goodbyes were reluctantly said, and we scooted off over the country roads following the excellent map drawn by Greg.

This was the route the locals used: follow the dirt road, ford the water course, turn left at a "T", take the next dirt road to the right, go four km and cross another river, pass Chateau Yalunda and come out on the bitumen. Soon we saw the Gawler-Lyndock road and the bright white glow of the Burge Marquee.

The marquee's interior was crammed with rows of long tables which were crowded with noisy chattering people. A barely audible guitarist played way off in a corner. Visible outside, through the marquee's clear plastic sides, the orange flames of a bonfire cast convoluted flickers against the black night.

As Sid and I edged between the rows of chairs and bodies toward our assigned seats, we were greeted by a young lad who had been friendly to us earlier in the morning. It turned out that our seats at the far end of the table were next to his mum. She and others immediately welcomed and drew us into non-stop conversation, eagerly asking us where we were from and what we were doing. We learned that the young lad had been an AFS (American Field Service) student and had lived for two years in the States. The mum had had two AFS students live with their family. Just as at the

Martins, addresses were exchanged, and welcomes and invitations poured forth on both sides; "Come any time...Our house is always open...Here's an address in New Zealand."

In between conversations the crowd sang along with the guitarists--*Tipperary, Bye Bye Black Bird*, and rousing renditions of Aussie ballads like *Lachlan Tigers* and *Waltzing Matilda*. One lady tapped me on the shoulder while I was standing in the food line and told me, "You get ten points for singing all the verses to *Waltzing Matilda*. You knew more verses than the Aussies!"

Finally we must leave and did so amidst many goodbyes, send offs, and invitations to return and visit. As we headed south on the road to Gawler into the moonless night, stars studded the black sky. Exuberantly we exclaimed to each other, "Wow! What an experience! That was wonderful! It was the people!"

I turned around for a last look at the bread loaf sized marquee glowing white against the velvet blackness. Our day at the Gourmet Classic had been rich for many reasons. But mostly it rang with friendship--friendship simply, straight-forwardly, cheerily extended. The tent's glow somehow symbolized the warmth and spirit of the strangers and friends alike who had embraced and welcomed us in that characteristic, open Aussie way. And as we drove away, that bright welcome glowed within both of us like the white tent in the night.

DEPARTURE

AS WE FLEW out of Australian skies, I was fine. Surprisingly, I felt little emotion. Memories and images popped in and out of my head--of people and places beyond the scope of the horizon. Lifting off from Melbourne's tarmac, circling over her stolid sprawl, I felt nothing. My affection lay beyond. Up there to the north, beyond the last line of green, were Naracoorte and "Wongary" and the Center. My heart was tugged by the land, not by the congestion below.

But I wasn't sad, was not fearful at the leaving. I felt close to Australia, renewed in it, and leaving did not destroy that closeness. Instead of wanting to cling to this land and the experiences of the last year, I was content, full of gratitude for what had been, for the seeds that had been sown. I left believing that I'd return in six months, and therefore the leaving was easy. There were other harvests to reap--in Oregon and in California--and I would enjoy that.

What did I leave with? With even more health. With memories of strength, endurance and relating with awesome nature through the use of my body. I felt gratitude for that health and involvement. I left carrying memories of places that expressed so emphatically the character of this boundless country--Monkey Mia, Uluru, Broome, and others. And, of course, I left with friendships--with people who had opened to us, greeted and embraced us in ever expanding circles of acquaintances and interactions. I took with me new awarenesses of a certain way of life as demonstrated by our farmer friends at "Wongary" and the station people at Curtin Springs.

I left reaffirmed in the knowledge that despite change, the country retained its attraction. People still had that open-handed friendliness and humor. Perhaps there were more areas of hiding it than before, but isn't that the current situation worldwide?

I left carrying a deepened recognition of how Sid's and my way of life worked. Because we were open to whatever opportunities came to us, we'd walked through countless doors which we'd had no idea existed 12 months before. Because we sought to give of ourselves, each from our different talents, we'd been welcomed over and over,

216

from referrals by friends to spontaneous meetings.

I carried in my heart, too, renewed friendships, deepened and expanded after 20 years. Today's connections were tender and shared in very different ways than when I was a girl in my twenties. I departed knowing that I'd made a difference in some lives, that I'd offered love and friendship and inspiration to several friends--new and old. I left very satisfied.

I left, also, carrying two basically finished manuscripts. One book done that I'd doubted I'd finish and one completely unanticipated "surprise" book. (This one!) I left as I embarked on new levels of sharing and interaction--for the first time I'd been interviewed on television, met with publishers, and had spoken about myself to groups.

I bid farewell to that vast country, feeling at once complete and unfinished. So much had come to fruition. So many evolving links existed with places and people. Yet, a whole side of the continent remained unexplored. A whole range of offered names and places awaited our return. So many fragments of experiences waited to be renewed and expanded. In some ways the year-end leave-taking seemed only the beginning--as if the more we got involved with Australia, the more doors stood open waiting, beckoning for us to fly back and sail through them.

I no longer feared losing Australia, or feared that leaving might mean a long delay in returning. That would be okay. For I'd learned to live so fully wherever I might be that I knew that whatever transpired, it would be wonderful. I left realizing that it *is* possible to come and go, to globe-hop, from year to year. I had finally released the old beliefs that said you make such journeys *once* or twice in a lifetime. So I no longer clung to Australia, desiring to stay, fearing that I wouldn't make it back for another 20 years. I was opening to a long-held dream--that of living half my time in the States and half overseas. I once thought it too unbelievable and impossible-- available only to the rich or clever. Yet look.

So it was a mixed leave-taking. The week before as we drove away from Naracoorte beneath the long tunnels of trees, the green paddocks sprawling rich and sheep dotted and crowned with massive gums, even Sid's eyes were moist. "I'll miss this country," he said for both of us.

At the same time, intermixed with the sadness, was the happy thought of return, of knowing that six months would fly and that once again we'd sail on tree tunnelled roads and sit and share with dear friends, would once more walk awed in the redness of the Center and be embraced into ever expanding circles of life and people of the land Down Under.

I looked back. A golden glow suffused the western horizon where the great land lay waiting, and we sped east into the darkening night.

Tree tunnelled road near "Wongary."

AVAILABLE FROM FOUR WINDS PUBLICATIONS

DOWN UNDER ALL OVER; A Love Affair With Australia by Barbara Brewster. $14.95 U.S.

JOURNEY TO WHOLENESS; *And the day came when the risk to remain tight in a bud was more painful then the risk it took to bloom.* Barbara Brewster's chronicle of her healing journey. $14.95.

DOWN UNDER ALL OVER photocards by Barbara Brewster. Moments and places in Australia as depicted in the book *Down Under All Over.* 6" x 4" mounted glossy color prints. Packaged in poly sleeve. $2.50 each. For a list of card subjects send request to Four Winds Publishing.

SHIPPING: In the U.S., including Alaska and Hawaii, add $3 for the first book and $1 for each additional title shipped to the same address. Books are shipped UPS or first class mail. Canadian orders, please add $4 U.S. for the first book and $2 U.S. for each additional title sent to the same address.

A gift? Just supply us with the name and address. Orders promptly shipped. Prices are subject to change without notice.

FOUR WINDS PUBLISHING:
P.O. Box 19033
Portland, Oregon, 97219, USA.
Phone and FAX: 503 246-9424.

IN AUSTRALIA DIRECT REQUESTS TO:
FOUR WINDS PUBLISHING
Box 236, Naracoorte
South Australia, 5271.
Phone: 087-62-3038. FAX: 087-62-3394.

GLOSSARY OF AUSTRALIAN TERMS

Akubra hat   made of rabbit fur, and seen on heads from all stations in life, the Akubra is as Australian as kangaroo or meat pie.

Backpackers   an organization which provides inexpensive lodging, often dormitory style, throughout Australia.

banksia   a native shrub.

bathers   swimsuit.

billy   a tin pot with a wire handle; used to make tea in over a campfire or to carry water, milk, etc.

biscuits   cookies.

bitumen   (pronounced "bitch-a-mun") pavement.

blackboys   native plant.

bloke   a chap, a fellow, a guy.

boab   a tree found in northwestern Australia; its bulbous shape stores water, enabling the "bottle tree" to survive long dry spells.

bonnet   hood of the car.

boot   trunk of the car.

bore   a water well.

Brugh Joy   an American doctor who teaches and lectures on the relationship of the mind, body and spirit in healing and disease; author of *Joy's Way*.

bush   the country; anywhere outside of cities.

BYO   Bring Your Own.

caravan   vacation trailer.

cavy   guinea pig.

century heat   when the temperature passes 100 F.

chemist   pharmacy.

chips   French fries.

chooks   chickens.

Christmas cakes   fruit cakes.

Coles   a nation-wide discount store, similar to Woolworth's

Corella   a kind of white bird.

counter meal   a substantial, usually reasonably priced, meal bought in pubs or hotels; eaten either at counters or at tables.

Great Barrier Reef	the gigantic offshore reef along the Queensland coast; famous for its beautiful coral and fish life.
David Jones	an exclusive and famous department store.
Devonshire tea	what one is given when one stops for a "cuppa" and the repast includes a cup of tea and a plate of scones spread with butter or cream and jam.
dim sim	a stuffed Chinese-style dumpling.
dinkum	genuine, the real thing.
draper	a dealer in cloth and dry goods.
drench	to give sheep medication.
esky	portable cooler/ice chest.
fairy floss	cotton candy.
fibro	a kind of fiber board used to construct buildings.
footpath	sidewalk.
footy	football.
fortnight	every two weeks.
Golliwog	a storybook character with a black face, big eyes and red lips, who wears black and white checkered overalls; Australian children have Golliwog dolls in the same way that American children have Raggedy Ann dolls.
grazier	a farmer who raises livestock.
gums	eucalyptus trees.
have a look	when an Australian says "I'll have a look," he means the same thing as when an American says "I'll check it out."
Institute	there is always an Institute in little towns; it is a public building where events, meetings, and entertainments are held.
jackaroo	an apprentice farmer--usually a young man; a jillaroo is a female farm apprentice.
joey	young kangaroo.
karri	a giant variety of eucalyptus found in the southwest of Western Australia.
left side driving	Australians drive on the left-hand side of the road.
loo	toilet.
lounge room	living room.
lugger	a small sailing vessel.

milo	a chocolatey beverage powder.
newsagency	newspaper and magazine shop.
op shop	thrift shop.
out the back	a frequently used phrase meaning "out in the back yard, lot, acre;" similarly used is the phrase "down the pub" meaning "at the pub."
Peter Panda	my stuffed panda bear who travels everywhere with Sid and me.
pumpkin	squash.
rissole	a fried meat or vegetable patty.
road train	a huge transport truck usually made up of two or three semi-trailers.
roadhouse	a petrol station which offers take-out food, supplies, and sometimes showers and lodging; often it is the only habitation for miles around.
roo	kangaroo.
sausage rolls	sausages rolled up in pastry.
scrub	the natural growth on semi-arid land--any undeveloped land.
smoko	means the same thing as a coffee break.
station	a ranch.
summer holidays	school vacation.
TAB	Totalizer Agency Board; it runs the horse and dog betting system.
TAFE	Technical and Future Education, i.e. adult education.
tarmac	pavement.
tea	dinner.
triticale	a hybrid of wheat and rye.
ute	abbreviation of utility truck.
wallaby	a smaller version of a kangaroo.
the" Wet"	the summer rains in the far north.
wether	a gelded male sheep.
willy willy	dust devil.
windswipes	windshield wipers.
Woolie's	Woolworth's.

223

SUGGESTED READING

Beadell, Len. *Too Long in the Bush.* (plus many other books by Len Beadell) Sydney. Weldon: 1965.

Bickel, Lennard. *Mawson's Will.* New York. Discus: 1977.

Blackwell, Doris. *Alice on the Line.* Sydney. Weldon: 1965.

Chatwin, Bruce. *The Songlines.* New York. Penguin: 1988.

Cleary, Jon. *The Sundowners.* Glasgow. Fontana: 1972.

Conway, Jill Ker. *The Road from Coorain.* New York. Knopf: 1989.

Culotta, Nino. *They're a Weird Mob.* Sydney. Ure Smith: 1966.

Davidson, Robyn. *Tracks.* New York. Patheon: 1980.

Davidson, Robyn. *Travelling Light.* Sydney. Collins: 1989.

Durack, Mary. *The Rock and the Sand.* Great Britain. Corgi: 1971.

Durack, Mary. *Kings in Grass Castles.* Great Britain. Constable: 1959.

Facey, Albert Barnett. *A Fortunate Life.* New York. Penguin: 1984.

Franklin, Miles. *My Brilliant Career.* New York. St Martins: 1980.

Franklin, Miles. *The End of My Career.* New York. St Martins: 1981.

Hansen, Ian, arranger. *The Call of the Gums: An Anthology of Australian Verse.* London. Adward Arnold Publishers Ltd: 1962.

Hindhaugh, Christine. *I Love a Sunburnt Torso.* Melbourne. Lorien.

Keneally, Thomas. *Brings Larks and Heroes.* Melbourne. Sun Books: 1967.

Marshall, James Vance. *Walkabout.* New York. Belmont/Tower: 1972.

Moorehead, Alan. *Cooper's Creek.* Great Britain. Four Square Books: 1963.

Niland, D'Arcy. *The Shiralee.* New York. W. Sloane: 1955.

O'Grady John. *Aussie English.* Sydney. Ure Smith Pty. Ltd: 1965.

Pearl Cyril. *So You Want to be an Australian.* Sydney. Ure Smith Pty. Ltd: 1968.

Serventy, Carol, and Harris, Alwen. *Rolf's Walkabout.* Adelaide. Rigby Ltd: 1971.

Shute, Neville. *A Town Like Alice.* New York. Ballantine: 1987. (Also available on video.)

_____"Kangaroos!" *National Geographic*, (February, 1979), pp.192-209.

_____"They Crossed Australia First, The Journey of Burke and Wills." *National Geographic*, (February, 1979), pp. 152-190.

_____"Sydney--Big Breezy, and Bloomin," *National Geographic*, (February, 1979), pp. 211-235.

_____"Western Australia--The Big Country," *National Geographic*, (February, 1975), pp 150-187.

_____"Australia, A Bicentennial Down Under." *National Geographic*, (February, 1988).

_____"Tracks Winding Back." *The Bulletin*, (January 30-February 6, 1990), pp. 42-120.

_____"North West Australia--The Land and the Sea," *National Geographic*, January, 1991.

*   *   *

NOTE: As of January, 1991, the sheep property of "Wongary" is functioning as a Host Farm and offers accommodation for guests. For information contact:

Diana Hooper, Box 236, Naracoorte, South Australia, 5271, Australia. Phone: 087-623-038. FAX: 087-62-3394.